GPS Outdoors

A Practical Guide for Outdoor Enthusiasts

GPS Outdoors

A Practical Guide for Outdoor Enthusiasts

Russell Helms

MENASHA RIDGE PRESS
Birmingham, Alabama

Copyright © 2006 Russell Helms
All rights reserved
Printed in the United States of America
Published by Menasha Ridge Press
Distributed by The Globe Pequot Press
First edition, first printing

Library of Congress Cataloging-in-Publication Data

Helms, Russell, 1963–
 GPS outdoors: a practical guide for outdoor enthusiasts/Russell Helms.—1st ed.
  p. cm.
 Includes index.
 ISBN 10: 0-89732-967-8
 ISBN 13: 978-0-89732-967-5
  1. Outdoor recreation—Equipment and supplies. 2. Orienteering—Equipment and
 supplies. 3. Global Positioning System. I. Title. II. Title: Global Positioning System
 Outdoors.

GV191.623.H44 2006
796.50284—dc22

Cover design by Travis Bryant
Text design by Annie Long

table of contents

DEDICATION

For my grandfather Orris Jennings Helms.
He was never lost

ACKNOWLEDGMENTS

MANY THANKS to friends and family who have endured a spontaneous GPS "lecture" or who may have accompanied me on one of my many outdoor GPS adventures. In the line of hardware, I would like to thank Suunto for their generous donation of the X9i. Steve Lovell of Garmin deserves kudos for his overall assistance in enabling Menasha Ridge Press to spread the word about GPS and units such as the Garmin Etrex models. In the realm of software, DeLorme has been generous, supplying copies of their TopoUSA program.

Heartfelt thanks also go out to the many guidebook authors I have coached in the use of GPS technology. Their success is my success.

Finally, I would like to say thank you to the fine folks at Menasha Ridge Press and a very special thanks to my wife, Linda, and daughters, Lucy and Cora. GPS may keep me on the trail, but they are the ones who bring me back home.

—*Russell Helms*

PREFACE

GPS UNITS, combined with topographic map software (see page 24), enhance any outdoor outing by assisting you with:

- **Planning routes**

- **Locating routes**

- **Navigating and gathering route data**

- **Analyzing route data after the trip**

Whether you're a climber, road biker, hiker, fly fisherman, trekker, or even a hot-air ballooner, GPS can make your next outing more interesting, less risky, and perhaps even more enjoyable. As you will read, GPS technology is at once fascinating, easily accessible, inexpensive, reliable, and useful. There are weaknesses, though, as with any technology, and those are covered as well.

After reading this book and familiarizing yourself with your own personal GPS unit, you'll be ready to hit the trail, plug into the satellites overhead, and experience a new level of navigation.

INTRODUCTION

NO ONE is more surprised than I am to be a fan of GPS technology. Getting outside (and usually getting dirty) is simply sacred, whether I'm scrambling up rock faces, trudging up steep trails, or barreling down single-track. Time spent outdoors is precious, and woe is the barrier that comes between my explorations and me. GPS units are extremely useful gadgets but need to be understood. Just as you don't want to set up a new tent in the dark, you don't want to have to figure out what GoTo means after you've wandered off trail and become hopelessly lost. In inexperienced hands, a GPS unit can make a simple outing an unhappy one.

To read any outdoor magazine is to immerse yourself in a culture of gadgets, gear, and gewgaws. Admittedly, there are extreme situations in which your life may hang on a bit of technology. But for the majority of outdoor enthusiasts and participants, less is always better. To me, Polartec clothing is the best thing since sliced bread. I have a medium-weight Polartec jacket that sees me through 95 percent of outdoor pursuits in chilly weather. But I've fared just as well with much cheaper acrylic sweaters from the thrift store!

What's my favorite outdoor activity? Although I enjoy riding my mountain bike to work, what really turns me on is diving into a

patch of thick woods and getting completely lost. If it's an area I'm familiar with, all I need is a water bottle, an energy bar, and a hat in case I'm out after dark. So why would I buy a GPS unit?

Because they're small, they're relatively inexpensive, and they provide the biggest tax-dollar bang-for-the-buck that I can imagine. When I switch on the GPS, I'm plugging into a multibillion-dollar satellite-based navigation system that is coddled in some manner by several of the largest and most powerful U.S. government agencies, including all branches of the military beneath the wings of the Department of Defense and the Department of Transportation. It's almost irresistible once you realize the

Trip Odom	Max Speed
1.84 ^m_i	49.2 ^m_h

Moving Time	Moving Avg
09 $^M_{IN}$ 30 $^S_{EC}$	11.6 ^m_h

Stopped	Overall Avg
01 ^{HRS} 24 ^{MIN}	1.2 ^m_h

Elevation
1046 ^f_t

Odometer
1.84 ^m_i

A sample screen shot from a Magellan GPS unit, showing a typical array of navigation data

enormity of what a simple $150 cell phone–size device can do.

This guide is designed to explain quickly and easily the wondrous possibilities and practical uses of a handheld GPS receiver. A GPS unit, coupled with inexpensive topographic-map software, allows you to preview your excursion, gets you to the jumping-off point, guides you along the way, and provides you with a visual record of your adventure much as a camera does.

On hikes that I've done dozens of times, I routinely take my trusty Garmin Etrex along, especially if I'm with other people.

"How far have we gone?" inquires hefty Aunt Sarah after a short uphill spurt.

With a twinkle in my eye, I reply, "Exactly

0.35 miles" instead of "I'm not sure" or "Probably about a half mile."

I could also rattle off a dozen other interesting details such as, "Our average moving speed is 5.3 miles per hour" or "We've ascended 38 vertical feet" or "At this pace, it will take us exactly three weeks to return to the parking lot."

On a solo day hike along the brushy West Fork Sipsey in north-central Alabama, I encountered a married couple and their teenage daughter walking in the opposite direction. They were on the trail and within easy reach of the parking area, but the looks on their faces signaled distress. It was pretty hot that day, and they had already beat out 10 miles or so. They were tired, and evidently the wife and daughter had begun to doubt their whereabouts. Was Dad leading them astray?

Glancing at my GPS unit, the man asked me how far it was to the parking area. I replied, "1.4 miles."

"How far, how far?" asked his wife eagerly.

"1.4 miles," I repeated.

"And this is the Sipsey River Trail, right?"

"Yes," I replied.

"And the parking area by the bridge is 1.4 miles from here?"

"Yep."

I've never seen such a forlorn group perk up as quickly they did, simply from a few bits of information. I may have even saved a marriage.

Can you head into the woods with a GPS device and expect to never get lost? No. The primary danger of a GPS unit is that it can and does fail. What if your batteries die? What if cloud cover and unfavorable satellite positions result in a prolonged period of signal loss? What if you drop the unit into a Class-V river? Well, you'd better have a backup plan.

As fascinating and useful as GPS is, you must still be prepared and able to navigate without it. The primary backup is the map and compass. A concise overview of how to use them begins on page 25. Using GPS will greatly enhance your understanding of the map-and-compass technique, but it's wise to hone basic navigational skills before or in conjunction with use of a GPS unit. An excellent text for anyone interested in learning more about map-and-compass navigation, or orienteering, is *Be Expert with Map and Compass* by Björn Kjellström.

When out in the field, you will develop your own style of GPS use. You may want to plot a course ahead of time, upload it to your GPS, and follow that. You may want to upload only key points of your journey such as crucial trail intersections, waterfalls, high points, or shelter locations. You may want to carry the GPS along without uploaded data and navigate without the aid of pre-plotted track points or waypoints. Or you may just want to have the GPS to turn on once or twice a day to check your position against a map. How much you rely on GPS data is up to you. Just always be prepared and able to manage without it.

PART ONE

GPS TECHNOLOGY

A BRIEF HISTORY

Atomic Clocks

PRIOR TO atomic clocks, quartz-movement watches kept the most accurate time. Quartz time, based on the vibrations of a quartz crystal, is accurate to about one-thousandth of a second per day. But with radio signals traveling at the speed of light, a clock that is off by even a thousandth of a second will produce a gross position error. Atomic clocks, accurate to within 1 second every 100,000 years, derive their precision from the highly predictable gains and losses of energy by atoms. These clocks, accurate to a billionth of a second, are key to the success of GPS.

Ancient travelers relied on celestial objects, such as stars, to find their way. GPS users also use celestial objects—satellites—to navigate. There are, of course, vast differences between a star and an earth-orbiting man-made object. You observe a star to navigate; a satellite is invisible to the naked eye, but you use its position data, or ephemera, to navigate. Modern navigators no longer have to wait for nightfall and clear skies, and, thanks to atomic clocks, they can receive precise position data continuously.

According to the National Academy of Sciences, in 1957 scientists observing the newly launched Sputnik realized they could predict its position by measuring the increase and decrease in frequency of its radio signal as it orbited the earth. This observation confirmed that a satellite's position in space could be accurately determined from the ground, which meant a satellite could determine the accurate position of an object on or above the ground, such as a hiker or a hang glider.

The orbits of the GPS satellites are designed to ensure that any point on Earth is always able to communicate with at least four satellites, the number needed to determine latitude, longitude, and altitude. Key to this ability to pinpoint an object on Earth, such as a kayaker, and track her movements are the atomic clocks aboard each satellite. All satellites in the GPS constellation continuously broadcast a digital radio signal, embedded with its position and the time. Basically GPS receivers lock on to these radio signals, compare the unit's time with the satellites' times, compute the differences, and then plot a position point.

To ensure the reliability of their position signals, satellites are maintained in 12,000-statute-mile-high orbits. Twice a day, satellite positions are definitively measured from the ground, and that data is uploaded to each satellite, which becomes part of its signal back to Earth.

Early GPS Endeavors

IN THE 1960s, two U.S. Navy satellite-based navigation programs, Transit and Timation, foreshadowed the success of today's GPS. Designed to locate submarines and ships at sea, the seven-satellite Transit system was opened to civilian users in 1967. Timation consisted of two satellites carrying highly accurate atomic clocks, which enabled scientists to accurately predict satellite orbits. The Timation satellites ultimately served as prototypes for the first NAVSTAR (Navigation Signal Timing and Ranging) GPS satellites.

Simultaneous with the Navy's satellite programs, the U.S. Air Force developed its own version of a satellite-based navigation system, System 621B. Not to be left out, the U.S. Army proposed a system known as SECOR. It became evident that someone needed to coordinate the various programs' goals and work toward a unified satellite-based navigation system. In 1973, the Department of Defense made the Air Force the lead agency. Within the year, the Air Force took the best of the best from the competing programs and developed the unified system, called the NAVSTAR Global Positioning System. Launches of NAVSTAR GPS satellites began in 1974.

Building the GPS Constellation

THE CURRENT GPS constellation includes 24 satellites, variously labeled Block II, IIA, or IIR. Up to half a dozen spares may also be in orbit at any given time. In addition to GPS functions, each satellite performs a variety of other operations, including the detection and reporting of nuclear detonations. According to the U.S. Naval Observatory, Block I satellites are "original concept validation satellites" launched between 1978 and 1985. Developed by Rockwell International, the 12 Block I satellites were given the satellite vehicle numbers (SVNs) 1 through 11. SVN 7 never made it into orbit after its failed launch in 1981. Designed to operate

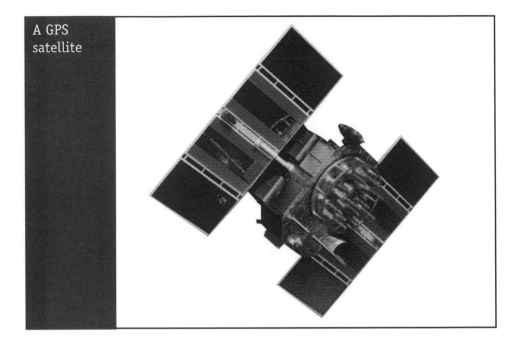

A GPS satellite

for only five years, Block I satellites are no longer in service. SVN 10—the last operating Block I satellite—was launched on September 8, 1984 and became unusable on November 18, 1995. Like the other unusable satellites, SVN 10 was boosted into a higher orbit and effectively disposed of.

Also developed by Rockwell, Block II satellites (SVNs 13 through 21) were the first full-scale operational GPS satellites. Launched between February 1989 and October 1990, Block IIs were able to operate for up to 14 days without contact from ground control. Of the Block II satellites, only one, SVN 9, remained operational as of this book's printing.

Block IIA satellites (SVNs 22 through 40) are second in a series of fully operational satellites. Launched between November 1990 and November 1997, with a design life of 7.3 years, Block IIAs can operate for up to 180 days without contact from ground control. Of the 19 Block IIs launched, 15 remained in service at the time of this book's publication.

Block IIR satellites (SVN 41 through 62), built by Lockheed Martin, are operational "replenishment" satellites. The vehicles can function for 14 days without contact from ground control and can also operate for 180 days in an autonomous-navigation mode. Each satellite carries three rubidium atomic clocks and, like the IIA vehicles, have selective availability (SA) and anti-spoofing capabilities.

The first launch of a IIR satellite failed, but the other 12 launched successfully and remain operational. As of publication, a total of 28 satellites remained operational; 24 satellites compose the primary constellation that GPS users rely on, with 4 backups.

Civilian GPS Access

AFTER THE DOWNING of Korean Airlines Flight 007 by the Soviet Union in 1983, the United States for the first time discussed making GPS technology available for civilian use, particularly in aviation. With the Department of Transportation leading the crossover of GPS technology from the military sector, two early civilian applications of GPS were surveying and aviation. Today GPS technology is everywhere, even in your cell phone. With the development of indoor GPS technology, shoppers may soon be able to precisely locate a can of green beans on a store shelf using GPS units.

Beginning in 1991, during the first Gulf War, the increased accuracy of bombing runs that GPS enabled demonstrated that the technology was an incredible adjunct to virtually all weapons systems. One political weakness of the early GPS design was its lack of designation as a weapons system. Block II satellites launched during Operation Desert Storm were positioned to maximize assistance to forces in the sky, on the ground, and on the water, contributing to the general success of GPS during the war. The Gulf War validated the value of GPS in modern warfare, securing its stature as a crucial budget item not to be toyed with. (In 1979, federal budget cuts led to the reduction of the satellite constellation from 24 to 18, slowing progress toward a fully functional GPS system.)

A shortage of military-grade GPS receivers during the war led to the military's widespread use of civilian receivers from companies such as Trimble and Magellan. To increase the accuracy of the civilian receivers during the war, which received only the C/A code and not the military P code (see page 12), the government turned off selective availability (SA) during the war. Selective availability degrades the C/A code, limiting accuracy for civilian receivers to 100 meters.

On June 26, 1993, the U.S. Air Force launched the 24th NAVSTAR satellite, which completed the network of GPS satellites, and declared the system fully operational in April 1995. Civilians have had access to the system since then but relied on the intentionally degraded signal until the military turned off selective availability in 1999.

In 2003, the Federal Aviation Administration initiated the Wide Area Augmentation System (WAAS, see page 14), a supplement to the Standard Positioning Service. WAAS significantly improved the accuracy of GPS position data, benefitting everyone from hikers on the trail to airline pilots in the sky.

SATELLITES AND SIGNALS

GPS: SPS versus PPS

ACCORDING TO a March 1996 policy report from the White House Office of Science and Technology, "The Global Positioning System (GPS) was designed as a dual-use system with the primary purpose of enhancing the effectiveness of U.S. and allied military forces." That purpose has been well established, along with a rapidly growing civilian-use industry. Developments in the military arena necessarily resulted in a crossover of technology to civilian applications and vice versa. With military budgeting a top priority of every U.S. administration, the role and development of GPS technology for civilian uses such as recreational navigation is virtually unlimited.

The complex and multilayered bureaucracy that maintains, develops, and deploys GPS technology is basically invisible to recreational users. But it's there working hard to keep the satellites in orbit, launch new satellites, and develop augmentation systems such as WAAS and DGPS (see page 14), not to mention covert activities that we might rather not know about.

There is one major difference between military- and civilian-grade GPS receivers. The military version of GPS is known as PPS, or Precise Positioning Service. The civilian- or recreation-grade GPS is known as SPS, or Standard Positioning Service.

In addition to the White House, three federal agencies govern the day-to-day use of GPS services. The Department of Defense maintains both the PPS and SPS networks, with the goal of providing continuous worldwide signaling; at least 24 satellites are kept up and running at all times. The Department of Transportation is the lead agency that addresses federal

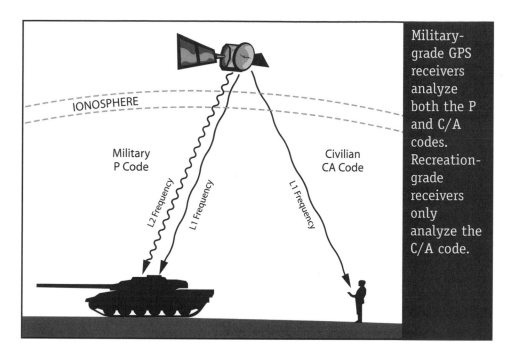

GPS policy and standards. The Department of State interacts with foreign governments and agencies to develop international GPS standards.

All GPS satellites beam military code—P, or precision, code—and civilian code—coarse/acquisition, or C/A, code—which GPS receivers translate into position information. However, only military receivers pick up both the P code and the C/A code. Civilian receivers only translate the C/A code. As a result, military receivers are much more accurate than their civilian counterparts.

The primary culprit that introduces error into position data is the ionosphere, the part of the atmosphere located roughly between 100 and 600 miles above the earth's surface. The ionosphere slows radio waves such as GPS signals beamed from satellites. Because timing of signals is so crucial to determining an accurate position, this slowing of signals contributes significant error to positions calculated by your GPS unit.

Military P code transmits on the L2 frequency. By comparing the L2 frequency with the C/A code's L1 frequency (frequencies slow at different rates), military receivers, can correct position error attributable to the ionosphere.

Civilian receivers must best-guess at the error introduced by the ionosphere, based on mathematical models of the ionosphere around the globe. The bad news is that ionosphere-introduced error compromises accuracy significantly, especially when coupled with more-local error-producing phenomena such as the earth's magnetic field. The good news is that augmentation technologies such as WAAS and DGPS (Differential Global Positioning System) eliminate much of that error, bringing the precision of position reporting much closer to that of military receivers.

DGPS and WAAS

DROPPING THE WORD *differential* in front of GPS indicates that corrective data is being applied to a coordinate reading received by a GPS unit. The most widely used differential system that corrects GPS signal data in North America is WAAS.

In 1996, scientists at NASA's Jet Propulsion Laboratory (JPL) presented a model for the first global real-time differential GPS. That same year, the FAA selected JPL's model as the basis for the United States' differential system, WAAS. Be sure that the GPS unit you purchase is WAAS-enabled, making it capable of positional accuracy of less than ten feet.

DGPS systems such as WAAS enable civilian single-frequency GPS units (like those made by Garmin, Magellan, Suunto, Lowrance, Trimble, and Brunton) to compensate for ionospheric signal delays. As noted earlier, military-grade units function on dual frequencies, making them highly accurate without DGPS corrective data.

Real-time Data Correction

WAAS IS a regional system that covers the United States, including Alaska; NASA operates its own global DGPS system. Local DGPS systems have been developed by the Coast Guard and by the FAA and may be used by civilians who possess the necessary equipment to process the localized correction data. As indicated, WAAS is a real-time correction. Signal data is corrected as you move along the ground, over the water, or through the air.

The WAAS system uses 24 ground stations positioned across the United States to supply corrective data to satellites. Ground stations are accurately surveyed and their precise positions determined. A GPS receiver at each station processes satellite data, calculates an X–Y coordinate based on that information, and then compares it to its own

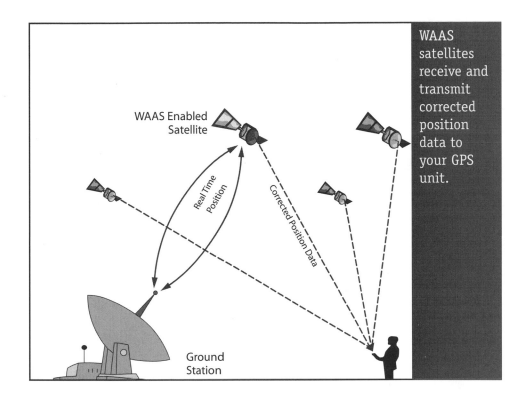

WAAS Enabled Satellite

Real Time Position

Corrected Position Data

Ground Station

WAAS satellites receive and transmit corrected position data to your GPS unit.

precise known location. The difference between the two coordinates represents the current signal error. That differential data is then communicated to two WAAS satellites that signal the corrected data back to the ground. A WAAS-enabled receiver listens to the corrective data and adjusts position reporting accordingly.

Post-processed Data Correction

WAAS CORRECTS signal data in real time, while other DGPS systems correct data after the hike or bike ride. Post-processing your own GPS data is possible but not particularly necessary for recreational purposes. Only survey-grade units collect the information necessary to post-process GPS data.

Satellite Maintenance

SCHEDULED SATELLITE downtime, during which signals are unavailable, usually correlates to maintenance needs. Maintenance of atomic clocks (a downtime of 18 hours on average) and repositioning maneuvers to correct drift from assigned orbits (a downtime of 12 hours on average) are two routine procedures that temporarily take satellites out of service.

Anti-satellite Attacks (ASATs)

SABOTAGE OF the GPS satellite network is a minimal worry for the recreational GPS user. But attacks aimed at any part of the system can and will compromise GPS-acquired data, whether you are engaged in an air battle over the Red Sea or straggling up Flower Mountain in Kansas.

As a recreational user, you can do nothing to predict or correct intentional signal interference, but you can be aware of the possibility (and it could explain why a trail you walked in Yellowstone shows up plotted in the Sea of Cortez). Anti-satellite attacks may cause reversible or nondestructive damage or may cause permanent damage. A simple example of reversible damage is the dazzling of a satellite sensor by remote laser. At sufficient strength or for prolonged periods, though, laser dazzling can lead to permanent satellite damage.

JAMMING

JAMMING OF a satellite involves either overpowering the uplink signal (ground stations to satellite) or the downlink signal (satellite to receiver). Jamming "drowns" the real signal without altering it. A relatively simple and inexpensive jammer can be built by most anyone, and there are even models available for sale. A simple jammer can drown out reception for GPS receivers within a 150-kilometer radius—probably not a problem for backpackers in Montana's Sawtooth Wilderness, but potentially a concern for GPS-reliant trekkers in conflict zones.

SPOOFING

SPOOFING A GPS receiver involves feeding it a fake signal that mimics either the L1 or L2 transmission frequency. The false information leads the receiver to report false positions and incorrect times. Spoofing is a step above jamming.

Needless to say, the military is highly aware of ASAT threats and has numerous countermeasures at its disposal. The greatest strength, perhaps, of the GPS-satellite constellation is its redundancy: if a satellite is disabled temporarily or permanently, spare satellites are in orbit, ready to take over business.

Fortunately, I think it's safe to say that the effort it would take to jam or spoof a satellite to disrupt a day hiker's navigation far outweighs any possible benefits. Any ill effects a recreational GPS user suffers at the hands of a saboteur is incidental.

HANDHELD RECEIVERS

THE CHOICES of handheld GPS receivers are extensive. Units range in quality from very basic to survey grade. For purposes of outdoor recreation, you shouldn't have to spend more than $300 for a high-quality unit. In fact, units costing as little as $150 provide all the function you will ever need to navigate, be it across a trackless void or the neighborhood golf course. One optional feature that is nice but not necessary is the color screen. If you have the bucks and don't mind the extra battery drain, color is a great option.

Good choices for beginners and advanced users alike are the Etrex models from Garmin and Meridian models from Magellan. In-depth information on these units is available online from both manufacturers.

The GPS Watch

THE SUUNTO X9i is the smallest GPS unit I've used and the largest wristwatch I've worn. I'm always tempted to speak into it or look at it when my cell phone rings. I'm singling out this gadget because of its newness and the benefits and problems it presents. In addition to Suunto, Garmin, Timex, and Casio also make GPS watches.

Such a compact device has definite advantages and disadvantages. First, its small size and multiple functions—it's a watch, weather station, compass, and GPS unit—speak strongly to the light-and-fast crowd.

You'll likely become frustrated, though, if you treat the watch as a typical handheld unit. To enjoy this tiny tool, you must use the GPS component sparingly: the internal lithium battery is mighty but will drain completely in about six hours with the GPS function activated. You can extend battery life by programming the watch to take readings at one-minute (versus one-second) intervals or by fixing your position manually.

For any outing longer than a few hours, you should anticipate using the unit only to spot-check your progress or to occasionally drop a waypoint for reference. The unit will function as handheld units do, providing

GPS units continue to shrink in size. The Suunto X9i shown here is one of several GPS watches on the market.

a GoTo feature (see Glossary), creating and navigating along routes, and logging and displaying speed and altitude data. But when using the GPS watch as a handheld unit, you'll need a reliable method of recharging it on a daily basis (see page 40).

The major shortcoming I've experienced with the GPS watch is the length of time it takes to lock on to satellite signals—on average, about eight to ten minutes until the first fix of the day is achieved. Once you've locked on to the signal, its strength often registers as weak and is easily lost. As with the handheld unit, you must hold the GPS watch nearly level with, or above, your waist to maintain the signal. I've found that walking poles (carbon fiber is best) are an ideal way to keep the watch oriented skyward without having to hold your arm in an uncomfortable position. The arm position created while riding a mountain bike is also conducive to signal reception.

When it comes to analyzing data after your outing, the X9i comes with Suunto's own GPS software. Topo maps aren't part of the bundle, but you can easily download your data onto a PC using the supplied USB cable. Once you've finished downloading, you can view geo-referenced routes, tracks, and waypoints, and you can even generate elevation profiles. The X9i also communicates with *National Geographic's* Topo!

software, allowing you to overlay your travels on top of digital topographic maps.

So if you're a minimalist or you need to know exactly where you are only occasionally, the GPS watch is a great option.

Carrying the GPS Unit

MOST OUTDOOR activities, such as hiking, allow you to grip and hold the GPS unit constantly. On foot, the simplest and most effective way to carry the unit is to hold it face up in the palm of your hand, at waist or chest level. Dropping the unit below your waist and pointing it at the ground almost always results in signal loss.

Other activities, such as paddling and biking, require a different strategy. Flat-water boaters (canoeists, for example) can attach the unit to the top of whatever cargo is lashed inside. Make sure you have it attached to the boat by a lanyard, just in case of an accidental dunking. White-water or sea kayakers have an extra challenge: it's unwise to lash any small electronic device to a boat that's bouncing off rocks or charging through 15-foot waves. In fact, it's generally best to keep the unit inside a waterproof case and bring it out only to drop waypoints (while scouting a rapid, for example) or check your position, as opposed to collecting complete track data.

Biking, especially mountain biking, presents a "gripping" challenge. The best way to carry an operational GPS unit while biking is to mount it on the handlebar. Handlebar attachments are designed for specific units, so make sure you purchase the correct model.

The mounting brackets are usually made of high-impact plastic that band around the handlebar. If you attach a unit to a mountain bike, make sure the handlebar tube is not too fat to accept the bracket. Most brackets come with rubber spacers to provide a range of fits. I have a bracket on my Cannondale for my Garmin Etrex unit. The bracket fits only the Etrex models and barely fits my fat handlebar at a narrowing near the inside of the hand brake.

On my first outing with the GPS unit mounted to my bike, I learned an important lesson. After barreling downhill through downtown Birmingham, Alabama, off the top of Red Mountain, I approached an intersection and a stop sign. To my right, strong wafts of burgers and fries drifted from a newly constructed McDonald's. I glanced both ways, then stood and drove down on the leading pedal. As I sprang forward, my left hand slipped and whacked the GPS unit, which flew right out into the middle of the street. Make sure you hear a definite click when attaching the unit to the bracket; otherwise, the unit may take flight.

When you're riding a bike, the various real-time bits of information displayed onscreen are fun to watch. The danger, though, is that the unit can prove distracting. So be mindful and try not to glance at the screen as you hurtle at top speed down a rain gully. You'll be able to safely check your top speed after you've stopped.

Initially I worried that direct contact to the frame would conduct the incessant jarring of wheels over rough terrain to the unit and thus damage it. My experience, though, has been that the bumps and vibration are not harmful. My Etrex has even survived hours of rough vibrations while bracketed to a push mower (so I could see how far I walked when mowing the lawn). Don't push your luck, though.

A REVIEW OF MAP AND COMPASS TECHNIQUES

AN EXCELLENT compass, such as the Suunto A-10 (which costs only ten bucks), is the most vital component of your backup navigation plan should your GPS unit fail.

Even without a map, a compass is useful to determine direction of travel, and it allows you to set and follow a bearing. With a map of the area, a compass will keep you on track and help you navigate. The map and compass won't provide you with a bundle of statistics such as average moving speed, but they will enable you to find your way just as well as a GPS unit. That said, you must know how to use the map and compass.

Compass

A BASIC compass consists of a magnetic steel needle that spins on a fine point while floating inside a liquid-filled housing. The needle's red end always points toward the magnetic north pole. The face of the housing is marked in degrees, with the four cardinal points—north, south, east, and west—clearly labeled. As depicted here, the circular housing rests on a clear, rectangular protractor base.

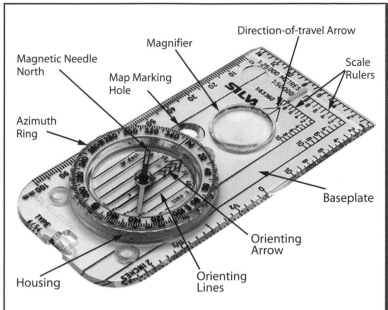

Magnetic Needle North · Magnifier · Map Marking Hole · Direction-of-travel Arrow · Scale Rulers · Azimuth Ring · Baseplate · Housing · Orienting Lines · Orienting Arrow

A basic compass such as the Silva Expedition 54 shown here is vital to have in your navigation kit, along with a hard-copy map.

The housing can be turned to align the underlying orientation arrow with the red end of the needle. If there is a distant point (such as a peak or tall building) that you want to walk toward, point the direction-of-travel arrow toward the peak, and then line up the orientation arrow with the red needle. This will be your bearing to follow, even if you lose visual contact with the peak. Just make sure you keep the needle aligned with the orientation arrow, and do not accidentally twist the housing.

When you need to return to your starting point, all you have to do is turn the compass base so that the direction-of-travel arrow points directly at you. The bearing you should follow is now directly opposite the direction-of-travel arrow. Do not adjust the housing. Remember to keep the needle aligned with the orientation arrow.

Since it's rarely possible to follow a bearing head-on without detouring around obstacles such as rock faces or lakes, remember these techniques.

First, rather than focus on the distant object such as the peak, navigate more locally. For example, look at the compass to make sure you are on course, then sight a large tree 100 feet ahead that lies directly in your path. Walk toward the tree. Continue the process until you've reached your goal.

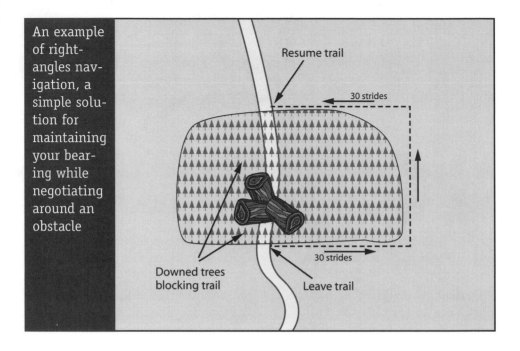

An example of right-angles navigation, a simple solution for maintaining your bearing while negotiating around an obstacle

Resume trail

30 strides

Downed trees blocking trail

30 strides

Leave trail

Second, you may encounter an obstacle such as a tangle of downed trees that interrupts your course of travel. To go around the barrier and return to your course, turn left or right at a 90-degree angle and count your strides. Say that you turn right and it takes 30 strides before you reach a point where you can continue forward. At that point, turn left at a 90-degree angle and continue until the obstacle clears to your left. At that point, turn left again at a 90-degree angle and take 30 strides. Turn 90 degrees to your right and you should be back on course, following the same bearing that you were before you encountered the obstacle.

Third, if you encounter an obstacle that you can see across, such as a lake, pick an object such as a tree and, keeping the object in view, travel around the lake and then directly toward the object. Once there, recheck your bearing and sight the next segment.

What if you've lost your GPS unit and have a compass, but you have no idea which way to go or what landmark to navigate toward? Well, you have two choices: stay put and wait for help, or try to make the most of the information you do have.

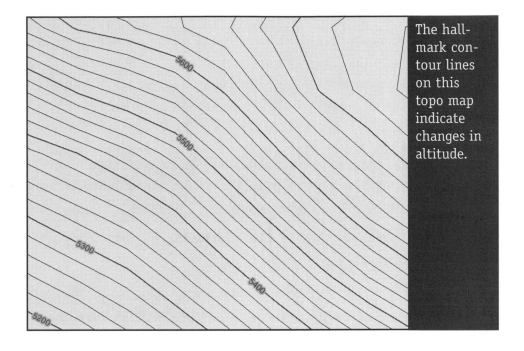

The hallmark contour lines on this topo map indicate changes in altitude.

Topographic Maps

THE HALLMARK of a topographic map, or "topo" for short, is the focus on the earth's surface features, both natural and man-made. Rivers, lakes, mountains, county roads, interstates, mines, and railroads are just a few of the topographic features found on this type of map.

Topo maps come in a range of scales, but the 7.5-minute series is the most widely used and, because of its large scale of 1:24,000 (1 inch equals 2,000 feet), is the most useful for outdoor activities. "Large scale" equals large detail for a small area. A 1:24,000 topo map, also known as a quadrangle, covers an area that is both 7 minutes and 30 seconds wide (thus "7.5-minute series") and high. In terms of land area, topo maps depict on average about 56 square miles.

Perhaps the most distinguishing feature on a topo is the contour line. The thin brown contour lines visually depict changes in land height. At the bottom of the map beneath the scale bars is the contour interval, the vertical distance between each contour line. In the example here, the contour interval is 20 feet. The slightly thicker contour lines labeled with numbers are called index lines. The index line labeled "5400" indicates a land contour that is 5,400 feet above mean sea level; every fifth line is an index line. Every line above that is 20 feet higher; every line below is 20 feet lower. Count up 5 lines and the height has increased 100 feet. Count down 5 lines and the height has decreased 100 feet.

A topo laid flat appears to be a rectangle that is taller than it is wide, even though it's 7.5 minutes "square." The act of flattening the earth's curved surface onto paper necessitates introducing some visual error.

The rectangle, or more properly, the quadrangle, is further divided into 1,000-meter squares, creating a grid over the topo.

Key information found on a topo includes:

- **quadrangle name**

- **road-classification legend**

- **state quadrangle locator map and grid with surrounding quadrangles**

- **north symbol showing true north, grid north, magnetic north, and declination values**

- **scale bars in kilometers, miles, and feet**

- **contour-interval value and survey datum**

Software programs such as TopoUSA, TopoQuad, Topo!, MapSend, and MapSource all use digitized topo maps. In programs for which the topo maps have simply been scanned and assembled (raster data), zooming in and out of an area on-screen is simply an act of magnification. The closer you zoom in, the less clear the map appears. Programs that use vector data for topo maps (meaning maps have been scanned and features converted into scalable graphics) allow you to zoom in deeper and more cleanly. With vector imagery, text remains the same size instead of becoming larger as you zoom in.

A topo map is best used in conjunction with a compass. But even without a compass, or having any indication of direction, a topo can be useful for navigation, provided you have some general idea where you are in the area covered by the map.

For example, you've hiked an established trail for several miles. After cresting the ridge of a small forested mountain, the trail disappears beneath a jumble of downed, burned trees. The hillside and valley below are devastated. A mile or so away, down in the valley, the forest begins again. *Hmm,* you think, conferring with your topo map.

After an hour of scrambling and walking on top of dead, burned trees, you're thinking you should have picked up the trail by now. But in fact, you've completely lost your bearing and have little confidence about continuing forward. You pull out the topo and judge north by the sun's position and time of day. Down in the valley, though, you can see very little of what is around you.

You turn around, retrace your path uphill, and become even more lost. You aim for a rocky clearing 100 feet higher and finally reach a point where you're high enough to have a 180-degree view of the land below and hills and peaks in the distance.

Without a compass, you are able to sort out your location by identifying three peaks in the distance that correspond to the topo map. You turn the map so that it points north, and with the sun's low position in the sky indicating west, determine that you need to head southwest to intersect the trail. It's rough scrambling at times, but sure enough, you do intersect the trail after 30 minutes.

The outcome is not always that easy. A featureless landscape or one riddled with narrow canyons can turn this scenario into a life-or-death situation. Luck, experience, training, and educated guesswork are always useful, but it's wise to carry along both a quality compass and a map of the area you plan to explore—and know how to use them.

Compass + Topo Map

COMBINED, a compass and topo map remain the navigation tools of choice for many people. Knowing how to use the two tools together is a key survival skill worth learning, whether it is your primary method of route-finding or your backup in case of GPS failure.

A basic protractor compass by a company such as Silva, Suunto, or Brunton will serve you well. USGS topo maps or similarly detailed maps are good choices. Be sure to check the publication date on the map: many topos can be as much as 30 years old and can contain information about features and roads that no longer exist. Ideally, you'll have a topo map that is relatively new.

Figure 1
The topo quadrangle name

A Typical Topographic Map

PERIPHERAL INFORMATION

"TOPO MAP" is a generic term for any map that depicts topographic features but most often refers to a set of 7.5-minute topographic maps (quadrangles) published by the U.S. Geological Survey (USGS). It takes roughly 54,000 of these maps to cover the entire United States. Beginning in the upper right-hand corner of a topo map and moving clockwise, much useful information is printed in the white space beyond the actual map. The following images are from the Fort Belvoir, Virginia, Quadrangle.

The title of this map is "Fort Belvoir Quadrangle"**(Figure 1)** It maps a 7.5-minute by 7.5-minute quadrangle of land. In this case, part of the acreage depicted lies in Virginia and part in Maryland. The "Alexandria" in parentheses indicates that the map directly to the northeast of this map is named "Alexandria Quadrangle." Although not shown here, the map directly to the east is the Mount Vernon Quadrangle. Dropping down

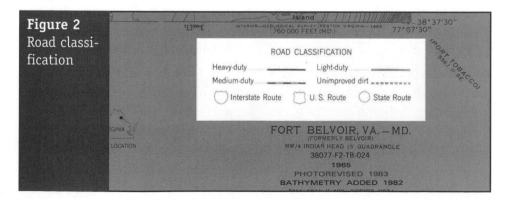

Figure 2
Road classification

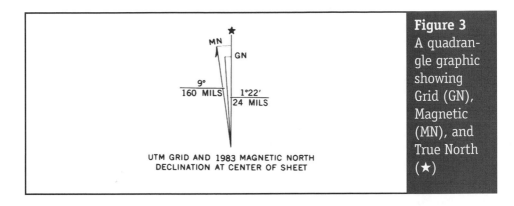

Figure 3
A quadrangle graphic showing Grid (GN), Magnetic (MN), and True North (★)

to the lower right-hand corner **(Figure 2)**, the map shows that the Port Tobacco Quadrangle is located to the southeast.

Under "Road Classification," a graphic indicates the different road types on the map **(Figure 2)**. Below that is data showing how up-to-date the map is. In this case, the last revision occurred in 1983. Moving left, you'll see a small locator map that shows where the quadrangle coverage falls in the state of Virginia, right on the border with Maryland.

Below the locator map is a small but crucial graphic **(Figure 3)**. The line with the star symbol above it indicates true north (the "top" of the earth where lines of longitude converge, aka the North Pole). The line labeled "MN" shows magnetic north and indicates that there is a difference of nine degrees between magnetic north and true north. Magnetic north is currently located several hundred miles south of true north and is migrating northwest. A compass needle points toward magnetic north, not true north. The line in the middle labeled "GN" shows grid north, indicating that the grid lines on the map vary from true north by 1 minute and 22 seconds.

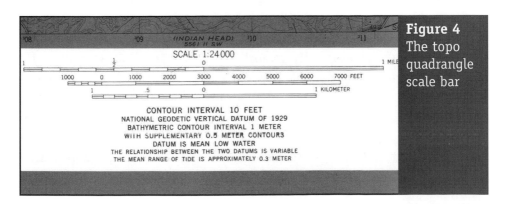

Figure 4
The topo quadrangle scale bar

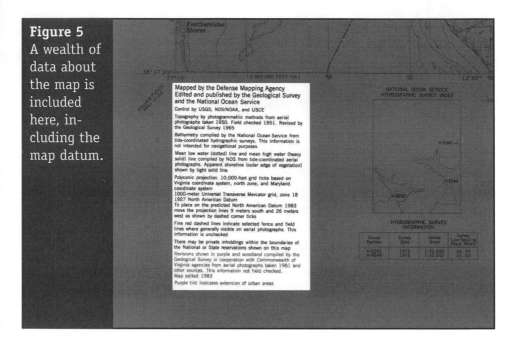

Figure 5
A wealth of data about the map is included here, including the map datum.

Within the figure:

Featherstone Shores

38°37'30"
77°15'   2 360 000 FEET (VA.)   '06   '07   12'30" '08

Mapped by the Defense Mapping Agency
Edited and published by the Geological Survey
and the National Ocean Service

Control by USGS, NOS/NOAA, and USCE

Topography by photogrammetric methods from aerial
photographs taken 1950. Field checked 1951. Revised by
the Geological Survey 1965

Bathymetry compiled by the National Ocean Service from
tide-coordinated hydrographic surveys. This information is
not intended for navigational purposes

Mean low water (dotted) line and mean high water (heavy
solid) line compiled by NOS from tide-coordinated aerial
photographs. Apparent shoreline (outer edge of vegetation)
shown by light solid line

Polyconic projection. 10,000-foot grid ticks based on
Virginia coordinate system, north zone, and Maryland
coordinate system

1000-meter Universal Transverse Mercator grid, zone 18
1927 North American Datum

To place on the predicted North American Datum 1983
move the projection lines 9 meters south and 26 meters
west as shown by dashed corner ticks

Fine red dashed lines indicate selected fence and field
lines where generally visible on aerial photographs. This
information is unchecked

There may be private inholdings within the boundaries of
the National or State reservations shown on this map

Revisions shown in purple and woodland compiled by the
Geological Survey in cooperation with Commonwealth of
Virginia agencies from aerial photographs taken 1981 and
other sources. This information not field checked.
Map edited 1983

Purple tint indicates extension of urban areas

NATIONAL OCEAN SERVICE
HYDROGRAPHIC SURVEY INDEX

HYDROGRAPHIC SURVEY
INFORMATION

Survey Number	Survey Date	Survey Scale	Survey Line Spacing (Naut. Miles)
H-9292	1973	1:10,000	.02-.05
H-9349	1973	1:10,000	.01-.05

"SCALE 1:24,000," located in the center of the bottom area, indicates that 1 inch on the map equals 24,000 inches (or 2,000 feet) in the field **(Figure 4)**. Three scale bars below that provide a method to measure distance on the map using miles, feet, and kilometers. Below that is contour-interval information. In this case the contour interval is ten feet. Counting up or down 5 contour lines on the map indicates a gain or loss of 50 feet. Continuing down, information on water depth is provided by the bathymetric contour interval, which is one meter.

Moving to the lower-left corner, you'll see that hydrographic-survey and reference data are included for those navigating by water. Next to that is a text box with the map's credits and notes about the map's projection and appearance **(Figure 5)**. The lines that read "1000-meter Universal Transverse Mercator grid, zone 18" and "1927 North American Datum" are especially important. "Zone 18" indicates the UTM zone, which a GPS unit uses to locate a given point. "1927 North American Datum" (NAD27) refers to the datum that the map is based on. Your GPS unit must be programmed to the datum indicated on the map you are using. Also, if you share a waypoint or track with friends, they must match their GPS units' datum preference to that of the unit used to gather the data.

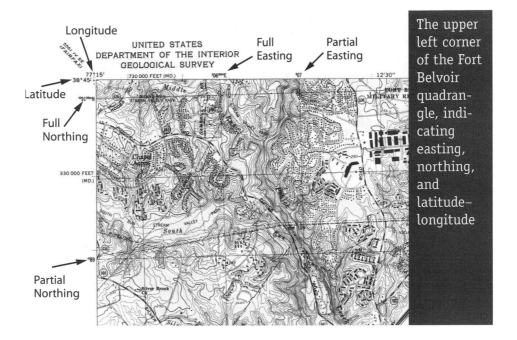

Longitude / UNITED STATES DEPARTMENT OF THE INTERIOR GEOLOGICAL SURVEY / Full Easting / Partial Easting / Latitude / Full Northing / Partial Northing

The upper left corner of the Fort Belvoir quadrangle, indicating easting, northing, and latitude-longitude

GETTING FROM A TO B

THE MAP, or quadrangle, is divided into squares that are one minute wide by one minute tall. Depending on the latitude, a U.S. quadrangle can depict as many as 64 square miles or as few as 49 square miles (as you progress, lines of longitude begin to converge). The "squareness" of the grid squares diminishes northward as well.

You can find your location on a topo map in two ways. One method is to use UTM coordinates; the other is to use latitude and longitude coordinates. Both are outlined around the map edges. Looking in the upper left-hand corner of the map above, you see that the latitude is 38°45′ (38 degrees, 45 minutes north of the equator) and 77°15′ (77 degrees, 15 minutes west of the 0-degree meridian that runs through Greenwich, England). The number $^{42}91^{000m}N$ located beneath 38°45′ is a full UTM coordinate. The number $^{42}89$ is a partial UTM coordinate. Down the side of the map, both grid systems are alternately referenced.

UTM COORDINATES

UTM COORDINATES index a specific point using a grid that has been developed for a wide variety of survey data. Some data commonly

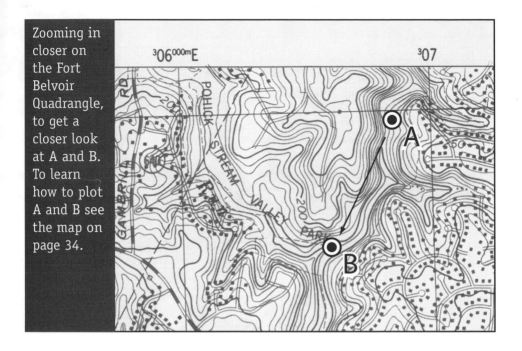

Zooming in closer on the Fort Belvoir Quadrangle, to get a closer look at A and B. To learn how to plot A and B see the map on page 34.

used to derive UTM coordinates include NAD27, NAD83, and WGS84. When using a GPS unit with a paper map, make sure your unit is set to navigate using the same survey datum as the map; otherwise, you will find yourself off course. Most USGS topographic maps are based on NAD27 datum, while newer maps use the NAD83 datum. Check the lower-left corner to verify which survey datum your topo map references, and then set your GPS to that datum (see **Figure 5** on page 28).

UTM coordinates consist of three numbers: zone, easting, and northing. The following example illustrates how to navigate from point A to point B using a compass, topo map, and GPS unit. The scenario references the map above, which is part of the Fort Belvoir Quadrangle.

Standing alongside a small creek at point A, you need to head directly to point B. Your GPS unit, set to use NAD27 datum to match your map, gives the following UTM coordinates for your location at point A:

Zone 18S

Easting 0306777

Northing 4290998

The zone number (18) refers to one of the 60 vertical zones of the Universal Transverse Mercator (UTM) projection. Each zone is 6 degrees

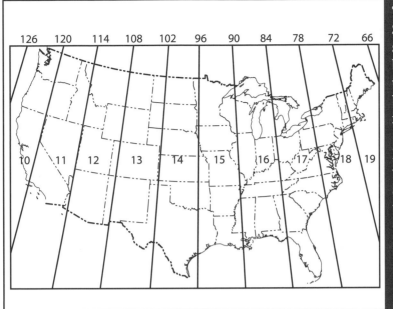

126 120 114 108 102 96 90 84 78 72 66

10 11 12 13 14 15 16 17 18 19

The United States is shown here labeled with UTM easting zones 10–19. Longitude values are at the top of the graphic.

wide. The map graphic above depicts the zones that cover the United States. The zone letter (S) refers to one of the 20 horizontal zones that span from 80 degrees south to 84 degrees north. The GPS unit will automatically detect and note the zone.

The easting number (306777) indicates in meters how far east or west a point is from the central meridian of Zone 18. Increasing easting coordinates on a topo map or on your GPS screen indicate that you are moving east; decreasing easting coordinates indicate you are moving west. Easting is plotted on the horizontal X-axis of the map.

The northing number (4290998) references in meters how far you are from the equator. Above and below the equator, increasing northing numbers indicate you are traveling north. Northing is plotted on the vertical Y-axis of the map.

To be clear, the easting number does not indicate the cumulative distance east of the start of UTM Zone 1; it references only its own zone's central meridian. Whereas the northing values for all locations represent distance in meters from the equator, easting values represent the distance from the central meridian of the zone in which the point occurs. The northing value is always tied to the equator; the easting value is always tied to the particular zone meridian.

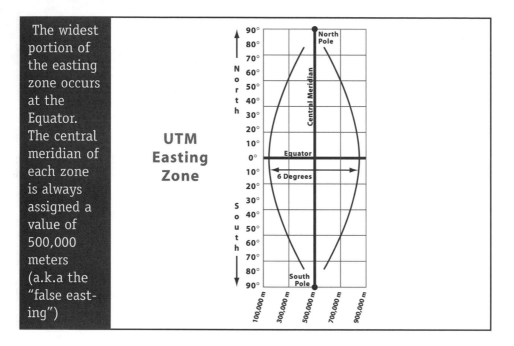

The widest portion of the easting zone occurs at the Equator. The central meridian of each zone is always assigned a value of 500,000 meters (a.k.a the "false easting")

Thus, a northing value of 4290998 indicates a point that is 4,290,998 meters north of the equator. An easting value of 306777 only references the UTM zone, which is 18 in this case. All UTM zones are 6 degrees wide. Imagine a line drawn down the middle of each zone; this is the zone's central meridian. The UTM values that run across the top of every topo map refer to the central meridian of that particular map's zone, that is, how many meters east or west it is. On the map on page 30, you can see that the numbers increase from left to right: 306^{000m}E (which = 306,000), then 307 (which = 307,000). But since a line that splits the zone references all values within the zone, points west of the central meridian *should* be negative and only points east should be positive. But to keep all UTM values positive, the value for the central meridian of all 60 UTM zones is assigned the value of 500,000. This keeps all eastings positive. If a point is 100,000 meters west of the central meridian of its zone, the value is 500,000 minus 100,000, which equals 400,000. The value 306^{000m}E (306,000) indicates that it is west of the central meridian, because it is less than 500,000.

FALSE EASTING AND FALSE NORTHING

An easting value is artificially based on the central meridian's "false" value of 500,000. For northing values in the Northern Hemisphere, the

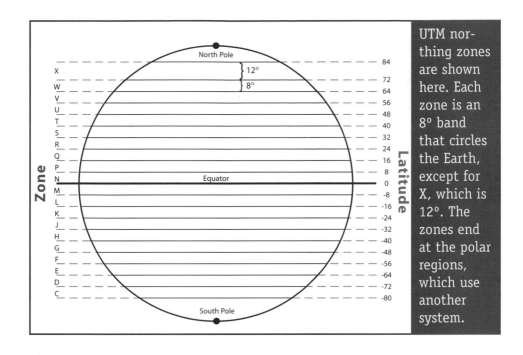

UTM northing zones are shown here. Each zone is an 8° band that circles the Earth, except for X, which is 12°. The zones end at the polar regions, which use another system.

equator is given a value of zero. But, as with eastings, to avoid negative northing numbers below the equator, the equator is assigned a "false" value of 10 million meters. Therefore, northing values decrease heading south below the equator, but they never become negative. When it comes to plotting your position on a topo map, the terms "false easting" and "false northing" have no import. The value of applying the "false" numbers is that in both hemispheres, increasing easting numbers always mean you are headed east; increasing northing numbers always mean you are headed north.

Now back to the scenario. Using your GPS unit, topo map, and compass, you need to travel from point A to point B. On the map, point A represents your location. A's UTM coordinates are:

Zone   **18S**

Easting   **0306777**

Northing   **4290998**

You need to travel to point B, southwest of your current location. If you have a base map to the area uploaded to your GPS and the topo features clearly mark the features of point B, you can pan down and drop a waypoint at B. You would then use the GoTo function to navigate to that

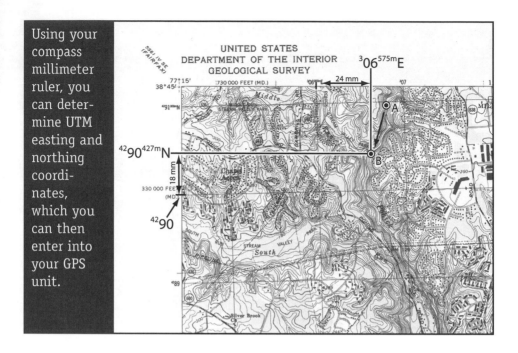

Using your compass millimeter ruler, you can determine UTM easting and northing coordinates, which you can then enter into your GPS unit.

waypoint, entering A's coordinates as your start and B's as your finish. You can also determine B's UTM coordinates by plotting the destination on a topo map using the ruler on your compass. Refer to the map above.

Mark point A on the map, and then draw vertical and horizontal lines (parallel to the grid lines) to the map border. The lines should intersect at B. The distance between grid lines is 1,000 meters. The last three digits of the easting coordinate tell you how far east you are of grid tick 06. To determine this distance, measure how many millimeters east that B is from the 06 grid line. Because the map scale is 1:24,000, 1 millimeter on the map equals 24 meters on the ground. Using your millimeter ruler, you find that B is 24 millimeters east of the 06 grid line. Multiply 24 by 24 meters to get the actual distance, 576 meters. Your full easting coordinate is Easting 306576. On the topo map, this is represented as ³06⁵⁷⁶ᵐE.

The last three digits of the northing coordinate tell you how far north you are of the ⁴²90 grid line (not marked on the map, but it falls between ⁴²89 and ⁴²91⁰⁰⁰ᵐN). Using your millimeter ruler, you find that B is 18 millimeters north of the 90 grid line. Multiply 18 by 24 meters to get the actual distance, 427 meters. Thus, your full northing coordinate is Northing 4290427. On the topo map, this is represented as ⁴²90427ᵐN.

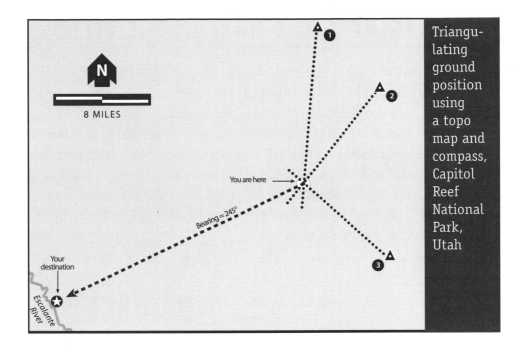

Triangulating ground position using a topo map and compass, Capitol Reef National Park, Utah

Enter the following full UTM coordinate into your GPS to create a waypoint on your unit for destination B.

Zone	**18S**
Easting	**306576**
Northing	**4290427**

Now use your GoTo function to navigate from A to B.

TRIANGULATING YOUR POSITION

If you only have the map and compass and no GPS (or your GPS unit has failed), the procedure to find your destination is the same. However, you need to find yourself on the map before you can get under way. A simple method is to triangulate your position. To do this, orient the map north, scan the terrain around you, and locate three distinct landmarks; these must be identifiable on the map. Once you are reasonably sure that the three distant objects are the three objects on the map, check the bearing on your compass against one of the objects, and draw a line on the map from the object along the same bearing. Do this for the other two objects, and extend the lines on the map until they intersect. The intersection will be your approximate location, point A. Now you can orient yourself toward point B, set the bearing on your compass, and go forward.

MANAGING A GPS UNIT IN THE FIELD

HANDHELD GPS units, as a rule, are tough devices designed for outdoor use. Most units are water resistant and can stand a quick dunk in a creek or the occasional jolt when you lose your grip. The upscale MobileMapper from Thales is completely waterproof (in one meter of water) and designed to take a fall onto concrete from 4.9 feet. Even less expensive units, such as the Garmin Etrex, are waterproof in a meter of water for up to 30 minutes.

Regardless of what you paid or how rugged your GPS unit may be, it's wise to exercise basic caution.

Water

BASIC MODELS such as Magellan's eXplorist or Garmin's Etrex series can be used in a steady rain. Battery compartments form a waterproof gasket when closed. Rugged plastic bodies, tough shatter-resistant screens, and sealed controls do a great job of keeping out rain, sweat, and other sources of water.

A simple, relatively inexpensive method to further protect a GPS unit from water is to place it inside a sealed plastic bag. In a pinch, a sandwich bag will do, but a product such as the Aloksak will keep the GPS dry and allow you a clear view of the screen through the tough polymer plastic.

If you plan to take your GPS through white water, anticipate a prolonged dunking, or worry that the GPS may be accidentally crushed through falling or impact against rocks, Pelican makes a variety of tough waterproof microcases. When I travel outdoors, I also carry a handheld computer and folding keyboard, which I protect with a Pelican microcase.

Impact

IN GENERAL, GPS units are tough and can take random abuse, but sustained impacts or a severe blow can disable them. I've stumbled and sent my GPS soaring through the air and crashing to the ground many times, but have yet to damage one that way. I have smashed a GPS screen by lunging into a trailside boulder while holding the unit. The unit continued to collect position data, though. A friend managed to

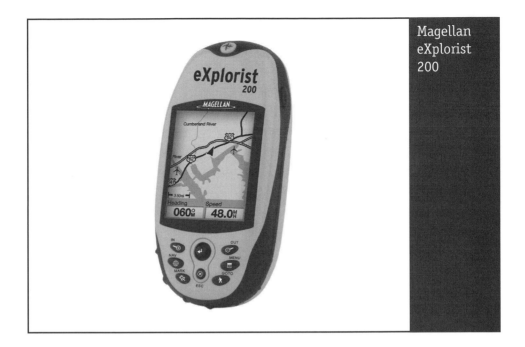

drop his and then put his full boot-heel weight on the screen, resulting in a partially damaged display. But the unit continues to work.

Mountain biking renders some of the most sustained abuse. This is a function of how you carry the GPS, how skilled you are on the bike, and the type of ride. To lock on to and maintain signal reception, the GPS unit needs to be directly exposed to the sky. I've tried a number of methods to carry my GPS while grinding out single-track, and none are completely satisfactory. I've stuck the GPS beneath the Lycra of my bike shorts (on top of my thigh) with fair results. The unit stays put but is annoying against my leg.

If you don't mind acquiring bits and pieces of your route and then piecing them together later within a topo software program, place the GPS inside a mesh pocket of your hydration pack or riding pack. Inevitably you'll lose signal reception more frequently, and dropping waypoints will become a chore, but you can focus your attention completely on the ride while you are on-bike. I have an older Jandd hydration pack with a convenient mesh pocket on the outside designed to hold the head of a tire pump. My Etrex unit fits in there snugly and orients skyward, but waypoint dropping involves stopping and finagling the unit through the mesh.

The best way to secure a GPS unit to your person while road- or trail-riding is to mount it on the handlebar. Mounting units usually accommodate a specific model, so be sure you purchase the bracket designed for your GPS. The brackets hold the units securely but provide minimal protection from a tumble. A front shock dampens vibration and jarring, making it easier to read the screen on a bumpy ride.

Cold and Heat

ALL GPS units operate within defined temperature ranges, generally between 5°F and 150°F. Extreme cold can affect the unit when you use it outdoors; exposure to temperatures below the accepted lower limit may damage the unit. To protect it, keep it in an inside pocket close to your body (along with a set of spare batteries) and sleep with it at night. With most commercially available units, you will not be able to collect complete track data under frigid conditions, but you will be able to pull the unit out on occasion to fix your position, correct a bearing, or drop a waypoint.

According to experience gained by scientists living in Antarctica, extreme cold poses three common hazards. First, LCD screens will freeze if left exposed, rendering a unit useless. Units must be carried underneath clothing and close to the body, and should be exposed to the elements only for position fixes, not for continuous tracking. Second, battery life is greatly compromised. The consensus is that battery sluggishness in extreme cold is unavoidable. The solution is to use the least vulnerable battery, which is currently the lithium-ion cell. Third, bulky gloves require that large buttons be adequately spaced for ease of use, thereby minimizing user error.

Protecting the unit from heat is a bit easier: just don't leave it in a hot car, lay it on a hot rock, or store it under conditions that may exceed its maximum operating temperature.

Dirt and Grime

HOT LAVA on your GPS is a bad idea, but don't worry about getting it dirty. Much less caution is needed than with other electronics such as cell phones. A well-made GPS is akin to a nice hiking boot. You can get it wet and dirty, but, like a favorite boot, it should be dried and cleaned often. It'll last longer and be less likely to fail when you really need it.

Each manufacturer provides general information on proper care and cleaning of its GPS units. Wiping with a soft, damp cloth is usually enough, but refer to your owner's manual for specifics.

BATTERIES

BATTERY OPTIONS may be the single most important feature of a GPS unit. The type of battery used, in conjunction with the power drain of your unit, will determine how long the GPS functions and even how it behaves toward the end of battery life.

There are two basic categories of batteries: rechargeable/nonrechargeable and removable/nonremovable. No choice is perfect for all situations, but there are definite advantages to being able to recharge batteries in the field and being able to remove batteries if the need arises.

Rechargeable Batteries

MOST GPS units can use three types of rechargeable batteries: 1) NiMH, or nickel metal hydride; 2) NiCad, or nickel cadmium; and 3) lithium ion. All three options are useful, but lithium-ion batteries are the rechargeable battery of choice not only for GPS units but also for cell phones, laptops, and other small electronic devices.

NiMH and NiCad batteries closely resemble each other in construction and provide the same general voltage. The primary physical difference is the use of metal hydrides as the anode for NiMH, and cadmium for NiCad. NiMH cells cost more and have a useful life that is half that of NiCad, but they offer 30 percent more storage capacity. The memory effect is a real problem with NiCad and occurs with NiMH, but only gradually. A NiCad battery must be fully discharged before recharging. A NiMH cell should be completely discharged every 25 cycles.

In my experience, lithium-ion batteries are relatively lightweight, charge easily, and power devices much longer than NiCad or NiMH batteries do. A lithium battery comparable in storage capacity to a NiMH cell also weighs around 35 percent less than the NiMH cell.

Another major advantage of lithium-ion over NiCad and NiMH batteries is the absence of the "memory effect." With the latter, the battery must be completely discharged before recharging, or it will "forget" its full capacity. NiCad batteries are most vulnerable to the memory effect.

Like all batteries, even lithium-ion cells eventually lose the ability to store and dispense electric current. But unlike NiCad and NiMH batteries containing heavy metals, lithium-ion batteries are less hazardous to dispose of.

Two types of lithium-ion batteries can be used in your GPS unit: removable and nonremovable. Units such as the Garmin Foretrex rely on an internal nonremovable battery. Charging is accomplished directly through the unit. For units with removable lithium-ion batteries, a separate charger is required. Lithium-ion batteries also come in standard sizes such as AA and AAA. These batteries far outlast NiMH, NiCad, and alkaline batteries, but they're more expensive and are not rechargeable.

Recharging Batteries

BEFORE ANY outing, make sure you have a fully charged battery on board. Don't guess: turn the unit on and check its battery indicator. If it's anything less than 90 percent, go ahead and recharge if you can. If you recharge or replace the batteries, check again to make sure that you have a 100 percent reading.

Depending on the unit you use and how you use it, battery life can vary wildly. From my experience, a basic unit without a color screen that does not display a base map will run continuously for 12 to 18 hours depending on the type of battery and how frequently you use the unit's backlight function.

As manufacturers ratchet up the features—such as color screens, base maps, bigger screens—battery life dips correspondingly. To offset larger battery drains with the more sophisticated units, lithium-ion batteries are becoming more commonplace. Unless the unit operates on an internal or removable lithium-ion battery, tailor your battery choice to your outing.

Just going out for a quick jog? Then most any battery will do. Planning on a weekend hike? A new pair of alkaline batteries might get you by. A set of lithium-ion batteries would be even better. If you opt for the NiMH batteries, make sure you have a spare set and also a backup set of alkaline batteries. Unlike lithium-ion and alkaline batteries, NiMH batteries fade quickly once the power is nearly gone. Alkaline batteries, though, tend to slowly dissipate, giving you plenty of time to prepare for an impending battery switch.

How about a two-week sledge-hauling expedition in Nova Scotia? You'll probably want to take a unit that uses either disposable or removable rechargeable lithium-ion batteries, along with a spare GPS that operates on standard AA batteries, plus plenty of spare batteries (mitigated by how efficiently you'll be able to charge them along the way).

GPS units save data using flash memory, which does not lose data should the batteries die on you. If you can, change the batteries soon after your low-battery indicator comes on. Save your track and waypoint data before you shut the unit down to replace the batteries.

Theoretically, you could start walking in Key West and, by the time you reached the Bering Straits, have never needed to pop into town for a fresh set of AAs—even if you had a cell phone, a weather unit, one of those stoves powered by a tiny fan, a digital camera, *and* a GPS. The key is recharging batteries using solar energy gathered and transformed into electric current by solar collectors. Solar-charging options are many, so you need to assess your outdoor-adventure tendencies, consider the equipment you already own, and factor in equipment you will most likely acquire in the near future.

There are two common types of solar chargers: hard and soft. The hard chargers, such as the C. Crane model, are typically boxlike and made of hard plastic with an array of protected photovoltaic cells on top. Batteries, 9-volts excluded, fit inside. A meter on the front indicates charging strength (as a function of sunlight strength) and enables you to more or less gauge how long it will take for the batteries to fully charge. With full, direct sun, it takes about three hours to fully recharge a pair of AA batteries. Weaker, intermittent sun will require six hours. A few cloudy days in a row will force out the backup batteries.

HOURS TO CHARGE WITH THE C. CRANE SOLAR CHARGER

	Weak Sun	Moderate Sun	Full Sun
D	18	12	9
C	12	8	6
AA	6	4	3
AAA	3	2	1

A soft charger, like Brunton's SolarRoll, is flexible in more than one sense. The tough plastic-coated photovoltaic array can be rolled into a

C. Crane solar charger

tube; plus, it functions as a direct charger or power supply for items such as cell phones, in addition to supplying power for a small charger such as Brunton's BattJack. Unrolled, the 9-volt charger (15.4 volts at 600 mA) measures 12 by 40 inches and weighs 10.6 ounces (4.5- and 14-watt rolls are also available).

The easiest way to plug into the SolarRoll is with a universal-DC car adapter. Most portable electronic devices, including cell phones and Brunton's compact charger, have DC adapters for car recharging. The SolarRoll comes with a female DC connector.

The clear advantage of a small charging unit such as C. Crane's is its simplicity of use. It will charge your GPS batteries and any other battery (except 9-volt), including AAA, AA, C, D, and GUM. The disadvantages are that you can charge only two batteries of the same size at a time, and charging time can be lengthy if the sun is shy.

The flexible SolarRoll tops the hard charger as far as the number of charging options (including internal nonremovable batteries), but the major advantages are solar surface area, shorter charging times, and the unique ability to strap an unrolled panel on the outside of your backpack and charge while you ramble.

Other primary considerations are weight and bulk, cost, backup power, and whether or not you'll need to charge removable batteries, internal batteries, or both.

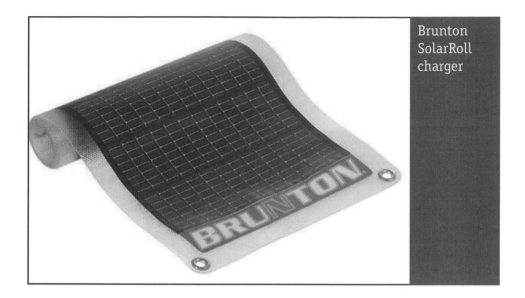

Brunton SolarRoll charger

Weight and Bulk

FOR AN overnight or even a weeklong trip, taking along a solar collector or charger is unnecessary. A couple of spare sets of batteries weigh far less than any recharging device and take a fraction of the space. One possible exception would be for the intrepid adventurer who sallies forth for a week of backpacking with three or more high-drain electronic devices.

For longer trips, especially to areas where batteries are not readily available, a solar charger just for your GPS unit is a viable option. What makes a charger more appealing, though, is being able to use it for other devices, such as a handheld computer or weather gizmo.

If you opt to go chargerless and weight is a major concern, take along lithium batteries, which are much lighter and pack more energy than NiCad, NiMH, or alkaline batteries. As an example, a single AA lithium battery (Energizer) weighs 0.6 ounces, a single AA alkaline (Duracell) weighs 0.9 ounces, and a single NiMH (Hitech) AA weighs 1 ounce.

Cost

COSTS ADD up on the trail just as they do elsewhere. A GPS unit may cost you only $150 initially, but other costs will follow. The primary expenditure will be power. A cheap set of alkaline AAs costs a couple of dollars and will last you about 18 hours on average, depending on the type of GPS unit. Rechargeable NiMH batteries are more expensive but, unlike the alkalines, can be reused. Sounds like a better deal? Well, figure in the cost of the charger and any adapter you may need; then consider how many charges you can squeeze out of your NiMH cells, and compare that number with how many alkalines you would have had to buy. Now do the math using lithium cells. *Bottom line:* if you use a GPS unit frequently, take long backcountry treks, or use multiple small electronic devices in the outdoors, then rechargeable is the more cost-effective choice.

Internal versus Removable Batteries

THE MOST practical approach is to assume that you will need to charge both types. GPS units and other small electronic devices are forever changing, so the flexibility of being able to charge both types, even if you don't currently own both, covers future purchases.

Without exception, any GPS unit you acquire that runs on an internal battery will use a lithium unit. These are rechargeable either with an AC charger or via a solar panel attached with a DC (cigarette lighter–type) adapter. The advantage is that you don't carry spare batteries. Internal lithiums are also very stable and recharge quickly. The disadvantage is the slim chance that the battery (if nonremovable) could fail and leave you without a GPS unit should you need it. You can cover the bases by toting a spare unit, but that's more weight.

GEOCACHING

WITH THE introduction of inexpensive handheld units, GPS technology has rapidly crossed the line from the serious business of landing jets and launching rockets into the realm of high-tech gaming. At its simplest, geocaching is a game of hide-and-seek. Geocachers stash logbooks and other items, then share a cache's coordinates (usually UTM or latitude-longitude) with others. The disabling of selective availability in 2000, which significantly boosted the accuracy of nonmilitary GPS units, has made geocaching more exact, and caches easier to find. The Web site **www.geocaching.com** is probably the best-known geocaching forum and source for cache-coordinate postings.

There are a variety of types of caches. The traditional cache is basically a waterproof container with a logbook inside. Geocachers who find the cache sign the logbook and then put it back in the container for the next seeker. Often finders will leave a small curio to make the cache more interesting for the next finder. Unless noted, it's generally OK to take an object from the cache as long as you replace it with another object (presumably of equal interest). Other types of caches include puzzle caches, for which seekers must solve riddles or puzzles to determine coordinates, and Webcam caches. Visit **www.geocaching.com** to get more-detailed information on the types of caches and to download the waypoints for thousands of caches. (As an example, you'll find more than 1,500 caches listed for Denver, Colorado, alone.) The sport is huge and is a great way to master your GPS skills while getting outdoors.

PART TWO

PLANNING a TRIP

PLANNING AN OUTDOOR excursion with the aid of GPS technology adds a little work up front but pays out well on the trip. For a trip close to home in an area that I'm familiar with, I'll consult a local guidebook for the basics or check the Internet for information such as directions to the trailhead or launch, trail length, and difficulty.

If it's a trail I've already collected GPS data for, I'll revisit the track and waypoint data, noting any crux turns, and look for possible variations on the old theme. On a familiar trail, I usually don't upload the track data to my GPS unit. If it's been awhile or if I have company in tow, it's never a bad idea to have the trail on my screen for reference. To upload data to a GPS unit, refer to your digital topo software's user manual. The process is very simple.

With the track uploaded, the cursor, which represents you as you move along the surface, should move along the track. It may stray a few feet to either side, but if the cursor steadily moves away from the track, you may be in the process of becoming lost (for example, the trail splits and you take the wrong fork). At this point, you should backtrack until you intersect the correct trail.

For new territory, using GPS to plan your trip enhances your knowledge of the area ahead of time, aids in locating the trailhead, limits surprises, and helps you select equipment that you may need to overcome geophysical objects such as rivers, walls, and canyons.

You can do a smart job of planning by using only a topo software program and a GPS unit, but hard copies of topo maps are also useful. DeLorme's *Atlas & Gazetteer* series, state-by-state collections of enhanced topo-map data, is a great resource to use at home and keep in your car.

A PRACTICAL APPROACH

FIRST, choose your adventure. Get a general idea of the topography by reviewing pertinent maps. Open your topo software program and search for a landmark near the trail, such as a town, lake, or state park. Locate the trailhead and known trailhead parking areas, if any. If the trail or route is established, it may already appear as a dashed line on the topo map.

With a good guidebook that includes precise maps, you can often re-create the trail on screen and save it for uploading. Although less accurate, if you have only narrative to go by, it's still possible to re-create the trail's general track on the electronic topo maps.

If you don't have enough information to draw your probable route, the next best approach is to plot waypoints at key areas along the route or trail. Place a waypoint at the parking area, for instance, and then examine the map for topographic features such as named overlooks, peaks, passes, gaps, lakes, and road crossings. Consult your digital topo software's user manual for specific instructions on drawing and placing waypoints on topo maps.

Once you've located and begun hiking, biking, boating, or skiing the trail or route, the track you create on the GPS screen as you move forward should intersect or pass close by the waypoints you've plotted and uploaded. The GoTo function is ideal for navigating between waypoints. See pages 33–35 for an explanation of GoTo.

A QUICK LESSON FROM THE WOODS

LOCATED IN my neck of the woods, the Sipsey Wilderness Area is a fine place to explore. The Wild and Scenic West Fork Sipsey River flows through it. Alabama's tallest tree, a 150-foot tulip poplar, grows there at

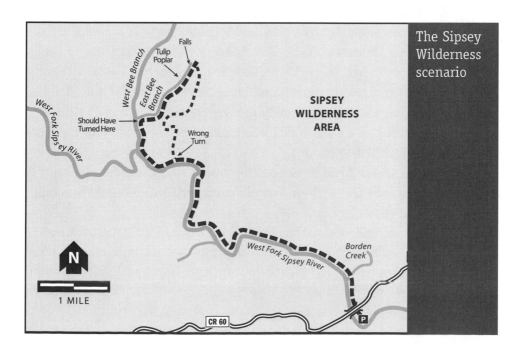

The Sipsey Wilderness scenario

the end of a unique box canyon. It's just a rich, wooly adventure every time I go.

Before my first hike to the big tree, I pulled out my Sipsey map, surveyed the area (some of which I had hiked before), and then visually followed named trails to my destination: the upper end of Bee Branch Canyon, where that tall tulip poplar lords it over the other trees. I had been warned that the turn into the canyon was unmarked.

Most of the trail follows the West Fork Sipsey upstream along the north bank, heading generally northwest. Prior to the trip it was easy for me to draw the track on screen, keeping my line close to the riverbank. I started the track at the parking area; then I took it under a bridge, along the river, and up to a point where I knew the trail made a wet crossing of Borden Creek just beyond its confluence with the West Fork Sipsey.

To put this in perspective, I knew from previous experience that no sign marked the trail's left turn across Borden Creek. On my first encounter with that particular junction (without a GPS unit), I walked right past the spot (and I've witnessed others do the same). I was looking for a footbridge and maybe a sign. I knew the trail turned left and crossed the creek, but I assumed the turn would be obvious.

After walking for a few minutes, I realized that something was amiss. I backtracked along Borden Creek and located the spot where the footbridge across the creek *should* have been. My expectation was to find a sign and footbridge. There was neither. It is a wilderness area, after all.

So I stood above the creek and looked over to the far side. I saw a slippery bank with several muddy grooves in it that led up the slope to what appeared to be the trail I was looking for. Now back to my more recent trip with the GPS unit.

With the track I had drawn on the topo map uploaded to my unit, it was easy to see exactly where I should cross, without needing the prompt of a sign or footbridge.

After fording Borden Creek, I picked up the trail as it ran upstream of the West Fork Sipsey. My next turn would be a right onto an unmarked trail 5.5 miles away that meandered up into East Bee Branch Canyon. When I drew the track on the topo map on my PC at home, I made an educated guess at the actual location of the unmarked turn.

As I passed scenic waterfalls and enjoyed pushing through the brushy overgrown trail, I began to ponder the meaning of "unmarked trail." At 3.5 miles, I passed the clearly marked Trail 202. The entrance to East Bee Branch Canyon was now only 2 miles away.

And then I doubted. With 1 mile left to the turn as depicted on my GPS screen, I came to a trail departing right. There was an old post that showed faint but unreadable numbers. Was this the unmarked trail that I had been warned would be easy to miss? Did *unmarked* mean no marker or just an unreadable one? The trail seemed to lead into what could possibly become a box canyon.

Had I uploaded the topo map in addition to the track data, I would have been able to discern my error by looking for the distinct pattern of contour lines that indicate a canyon. What I had decided to hike into was not a canyon.

Also—and crucial for any outdoor outing—I should have brought the hard-copy map of the area with me. I had a very good map of the area but had accidentally left it in the trunk of my car! The map would have helped me decide that this unclearly marked junction was not the entrance to East Bee Branch Canyon.

So I ignored what my GPS showed me, which was correct, and headed uphill about a mile too early. Having never been into the canyon, I did not know what to expect initially. After a half mile or so, though, I noticed that the line I was walking nearly paralleled the track I had uploaded. But this was no canyon. The trail climbed and wound to the top of a bluff and then headed north.

Figuring I would wind up somewhere above the canyon, I kept walking. Sure enough, I soon reached a trail fork, bore left, and shortly found myself standing above the 75-foot falls at the head of East Bee Branch Canyon. The track I had just created while walking now met with the terminus of the track I had uploaded.

I was never really lost or in any distress, but I learned a few things. First, topo maps, although not perfect, are very useful. Had I uploaded the actual map along with the track I had drawn, I would have waited and made the correct turn. Second, I had actually drawn the correct track, even though I was making an educated guess. Had I followed that, I would have made the correct turn as well, even without the contour lines of the topo map. Third, I should have taken a hard-copy map as backup to assist with navigation.

SIDE TRIPS

IN ADDITION to plotting your course, locating and marking key geonavigational objects (such as overlooks, lakes, creek inflows, and trail–road intersections), and identifying overnight-camping spots, GPS technology lets you plan ahead and plot points of interest you'll encounter along the way.

Let's say you're paddling a section of the Chattahoochee River near Atlanta and you know the best crab fritter this side of heaven is to be had just a hundred feet or so off the west bank. You can drop a waypoint on the topo map and then draw the track from the river right to the front door of some good eating. By watching your GPS unit as you paddle, you'll know exactly how far you are from the takeout, how fast you're headed there, and how long it will take you to reach the takeout at your current speed.

And likewise for any other trip, drop waypoints for off-trail waterfalls, a country store that sells ice cream, a haunted fire tower, or any other feature on the map that catches your eye as a possible side venture.

CONTINGENCY

WHEN YOU'RE undertaking journeys that have specific destinations, such as a mountain peak, it is reasonable to preview the territory you'll visit, noting alternative routes to your goal and routes that may be used to exit the area should the need arise.

You can draw alternative routes or waypoints that mark key geographic features or trail intersections and upload these to your unit along with the planned route—just in case.

INFORMATION

WHILE YOU'RE plopped in front of your PC and perusing digital maps prior to your adventure, there is a wealth of data available to analyze and mull over.

Along with the visual data, the program determines a variety of elevation and distance measurements. You can draw the track you intend to

Use your GPS unit to navigate to the trailhead.

follow, possible side trips, and "just in case" escape routes; then you can look over an array of data about those routes, including mileage, elevation gain, and elevation loss.

Paper topo maps provide this data, but it's obtained more easily with a digital topo map in a program such as TopoUSA, Topo!, or MapSource.

GETTING TO THE TRAILHEAD

MANY PEOPLE get their first glimpse of a GPS unit inside a car, truck, boat, or airplane. An onboard GPS unit functions in the same way as a handheld unit: it tells you where you are and where you're headed, and, when loaded with street-level software, can give you verbal turn-by-turn directions as you drive. So, if you don't have an onboard GPS in your vehicle, you can use your handheld GPS to navigate right to the trailhead or other launching point for your next adventure.

If you know where the trailhead is located, the easiest way to navigate directly to it is to have your topo software program draw the most efficient route. Using the Route feature, drop a start icon at your point of departure and an end icon at your destination. The program will then calculate the shortest route and draw it on-screen. You can upload the route to your GPS unit and print out turn-by-turn directions. Remember to match your software's survey datum with the datum that your unit is set up to use (see page 28).

If the trailhead or launch is some distance from the parking area, you can drop a waypoint onto your digital topo map and upload that single waypoint to your GPS. Once you've parked, use the unit's GoTo feature to guide you to the trailhead. If all you have is a paper topo map, you can create a waypoint on your GPS by manually entering the UTM coordinates (zone, easting, and northing). You obtain the coordinates by reading the grid numbers on the topo map (see page 34) and typing them into your unit using the built-in text-typing feature. Then use the GoTo function to take you there.

PART THREE

NAVIGATING

and

GATHERING
TRAIL DATA

SO YOU HAVE a couple of days off and a nearby wilderness area is calling your name. You've done your research, reviewed your proposed path of travel with your topo software, uploaded the route to find the parking area nearest the trailhead or launch you plan to use, and uploaded or entered the UTM coordinates of the actual trailhead (or your best guess). You have a spare set of batteries, a manual compass, and a hard-copy topo map of the area, all to back up your GPS unit. Fast-forward, and there you are standing at the trailhead. In fact, a sign reads "Trail 101." From here you know that what lies ahead is an 14-mile loop that takes you northeast through a hardwood forest, then northwest up and over a 4,000-foot mountain, then southwest through a narrow river canyon, and finally southeast through a flat, boggy area, back to the trailhead.

DAY ONE

IT'S LATE MAY, warm during the day, chilly at night. Two friends, Nate and Darlene, are with you for the two-day hike. The plan is to hike through the forest, cross the mountain at its high point, and camp about halfway down the other side at a landmark called Turtle Rock. The first day's hike is 7.2 miles, leaving 6.8 miles for the second day.

Because the trail is established, you haven't uploaded the actual track you will be walking, but you have uploaded six waypoints from your digital topo-map program onto your GPS unit. The waypoints mark crucial landmarks, providing confidence along the journey that you are indeed taking the right path.

Waypoints

01 Trailhead

02 Junction with Trail 105

03 Mountain high point

04 Turtle Rock

05 Intersect river

06 Cemetery

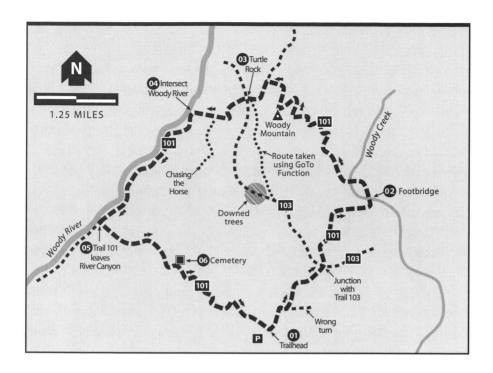

Getting Started, Late

IT'S 2 P.M. You had planned on hitting the trail by 10 a.m., but Nate slept late and Darlene insisted on stopping and purchasing lottery tickets just across the state line. Then it was lunchtime, and another hour was lost at a fast-food place. Having the route to the trailhead uploaded to the unit kept you from getting lost, though.

With the GPS unit locked on to several satellites and the track log activated, you begin the hike, relieved to be on the trail. It feels good to be out beneath the blue sky. Walking briskly, the group chats away, working up a mild sweat. On the GPS screen, your progress is already an inch-long line heading northeast. At the current zoom level, you can't see the first waypoint, but it will come into view when you're a mile or so away from it.

On the Wrong Trail

THE TRAIL seems to narrow suddenly and then kind of disappears. In the excitement of getting under way, somehow you made a wrong turn. You think. First you zoom out to increase the area shown on the screen.

Waypoint 02, the junction with Trail 105, comes into view, and you notice that your current track is headed too far east.

Turning around, you guide Nate and Darlene back along the path you've been hiking, looking for the point where you headed in the wrong direction. Within ten minutes, you reach a small clearing, look over to the right, and notice another trail. It heads off into the woods along a contour line. After just a few minutes, it's obvious that you are back on an established path and that it's leading you much more directly to Waypoint 02.

After an hour or so, you've hiked a total of 1.5 miles, not including the unexpected detour. At this rate it will take you another four hours to reach Turtle Rock. Suddenly a trail crosses the one you're walking on. You look at your GPS screen and notice that this is not Trail 105. It is unmarked, but this is probably Trail 103, a shortcut to Turtle Rock.

To check, you bring out the topo map and find your location. It looks like this is Trail 103. To be sure, you check the UTM coordinates of your current location on the GPS unit. The topo map was produced using NAD27 datum, and your unit is set to use NAD27 as well. By finding the easting number at the top of the map, then the northing number on the side (see page 34), you determine your exact position and confirm that this is indeed Trail 103.

A Route Change

AFTER DISCUSSING the situation with Nate and Darlene, who are hungry and beginning to whine just a bit, you decide it's best to take the shortcut to Turtle Rock. Otherwise you'll be hiking in the dark (you've confirmed that the moon will be only a thin sliver using the sun-and-moon function on the GPS unit) and will have to set up camp in the dark. To keep on schedule and avoid a bad camping experience—and few things are worse than a bad camping experience—you decide Trail 103 is the answer. According to the topo map, it skirts around to Turtle Rock rather than traveling over the mountain. It's only 3 miles away. Perfect.

Nate and Darlene's spirits pick up tremendously, and talk turns to a bag of chili Nate has in his backpack. The trail has ceased to climb and all seems well when the trail crests a small ridge and enters a huge tangle of dead trees, maybe a hundred acres. The trail is all but buried. It looks like pine beetles have wreaked havoc and trees have been felled and left to rot.

Without hesitating, you fire up your GPS unit's GoTo function. From your current location, you instruct the unit to lead you to Waypoint 04, Turtle Rock. The Navigation screen points you directly there. All you have to do is follow a bearing of 340 degrees, almost due north, for 1.5 miles. You double-check this information against the topo map. On the map, the trail from your current location does not actually make a beeline for Turtle Rock but follows a contour line, taking it in a gentle curve.

Surveying the mess of downed trees, you realize that a straight path to Turtle Rock is not possible. So, relying on the navigation screen, you lead the group in the general direction, following the path of least resistance. As you monitor the navigation screen, it's easy to see how far off course you are and which way you need to turn to resume your desired bearing of 340 degrees. Soon the downed trees thin, and up ahead you can see what looks like Turtle Rock sitting in a field of boulders. Trail 103 also reappears, and you follow it right up to a large campfire ring at the base of the overhanging Turtle Rock. Trail 101 is a few yards away. It's 5 p.m., just enough time to pitch tents and get the chili going before night falls.

DAY TWO

THE CHILI was fantastic, but separate tents that night would have been nice. After having coffee and some honey buns Darlene picked up at the convenience store where she bought the lottery tickets, you lead the group southwest toward Waypoint 05, where Trail 101 meets the river about 1 mile away.

Off-the-trail Excitement

WITH A HALF-MILE under your boots, Nate shouts, "A deer!" He promptly leaves the trail to get a closer look. Darlene follows and so do you. No one can see the deer, but Nate really wants to try and get a closer look. You decide it would be easier if everyone took off their packs and continued. With the GPS, you know you can backtrack easily to the packs and the trail. Before continuing, you drop a waypoint to mark the packs' location.

After 30 minutes, the terrain becomes steep, and interest in the mysterious deer dissipates. You look down at the GPS unit, and the screen is blank. The batteries have died. The spare set is in your backpack. Out come the topo map and compass. By comparing terrain features in the distance with features on the topo map and having a general idea of where you are, you decide to follow a nearly due-south bearing. This will definitely get you back to the trail, but you may miss the packs. As a precaution, you, Nate, and Darlene fan out, keeping within ten feet or so of each other as you each follow the same bearing, walking parallel to one another. Within a few minutes, Darlene sights the packs. You load new batteries into the GPS and resume the hike back to Trail 101.

Satellite Reception Fails

AS YOU draw close to the river, the sky begins to cloud and the GPS loses satellite contact every few minutes, leaving gaps in the track drawn on the screen. The trail winds down beside the slow-moving, 20-foot-wide river and follows it downstream to the southeast. A canyon wall to your left gradually grows to a height of 80 to 100 feet, wreaking havoc on satellite reception. Since the trail follows the river, you decide to turn off the unit and wait until you climb out of the canyon.

A light rain begins to fall, and you take off your glasses. It's still pleasant, just a minor inconvenience. The group has walked in silence for an hour or so when Nate asks if that trail about half a mile back was the one you should have taken. Luckily, the GPS locks on to a sufficiently strong signal, and you see that Nate is right: Waypoint 05 is now behind you. Trail 101 turned left. Shortly, though, all is well. Trail 101 is regained, and the group is out of the canyon. A strong satellite signal has also returned.

Alive and Well

AFTER A quick lunch of beef jerky and apples, you reach Waypoint 06, the cemetery. The small family plot holds several graves from the late 19th and early 20th centuries. Only 1.4 miles to go.

Back at the parking lot, your tired but happy group piles into the minivan and immediately starts discussing the next outing. On the drive home, you decide to give your GPS unit a nickname.

PART FOUR

ANALYZING TRAIL DATA after the TRIP

AFTER A TRIP, even a short one, it's nice to reflect. The most common method of reflection on a journey is probably photography. More than likely, you had a nice time. Even if you wound up flipping your canoe, twisting your ankle, or arguing with your buddy over the proper way to extinguish a campfire, you'll want to look at the pictures and hopefully laugh it off.

Similar to keeping a journal, capturing a GPS log of your trip provides a cartographic record of your adventure. On the ground, weaving among tall pines, mountain biking along rocky back roads, or inching your way up a big wall, the experience lays down a track of images in your mind as well as a track on your GPS unit. Back at home, watching your path of travel appear in its proper place on top of a topo map is mildly magical. You immediately see where you took the wrong path and lost an hour of daylight backtracking. The first night's camp is labeled with a waypoint. Another waypoint marks the nest of yellow jackets that you disturbed with your hiking pole. You follow the line up and over ridges, along rivers, across roads, and back to the trailhead. It's a good feeling. Having gathered the data, make sure you save your track and waypoint files so you can easily locate them for future use.

Worth noting again, though, are the inevitable measurement errors that will be incorporated into your data. For example, if your path took you along a narrow river for several miles, you may notice that your downloaded track sometimes crosses the river where you did not cross. Most topo software programs allow you to edit and redraw the track as needed. Just be aware that, as with a photo or journal, you may need to clean up and edit your GPS data.

CONTRIBUTIONS TO GPS ERROR

MANY FACTORS can affect the accuracy of position data received by GPS units. Fortunately, the information is almost always accurate enough for outdoor pursuits such as kayaking, backpacking, and biking. Of course, you would never completely trust navigation to only a GPS device. But using it in conjunction with a map and compass as backup and practicing general common sense, you'll find that the data acquired by your recreational GPS unit will always be enough to direct you home.

Sources of error can be divided into four camps, only three of which should ever be of concern to you (unless you pursue spying as a career): 1) the user, 2) the environment, 3) the system, and 4) the enemy.

User Error

USER ERROR sounds mundane but can seriously affect how cleanly and accurately tracks and waypoints are laid down. The primary user error is as simple as handling the unit sloppily. If you keep the unit in your pocket, hold it down by your leg with the antenna pointing toward the ground, or otherwise physically interfere with signal reception, the data will be compromised. Likewise, don't carry other electronic devices (for instance, a handheld cassette recorder) close to the unit. Not all cases of signal loss are due to user handling, but many are.

Environmental Error

ENVIRONMENTAL sources are the most common and most significant sources of data error. Two primary environmental sources of error are the earth's ionosphere and magnetic field. The ionosphere slows satellite signals, but at varying rates depending on a variety of factors. Military-grade receivers correct ionospheric error by analyzing the difference between P code (L1 frequency) and C/A code (L2 frequency) delays. Civilian receivers only process C/A codes. For more on how civilian-grade receivers overcome much of the ionospheric error, see page 12.

The earth's magnetic field has been weakening over millennia, and scientists predict that the molten core of our planet may alter to such a degree in the near future that the North and South poles will actually reverse. Now that will be a bad day for GPS navigation (and an orienteering event). According to the National Oceanic and Atmospheric Administration (NOAA), the magnetic field is the most significant factor for GPS operations within the continental United States. Abrupt disturbances in this field are not perceptible to us, but you can check on disturbances by clicking on the Planetary K-Index Plot link located at **www.sel.noaa.gov/nav/gps.html.** In Canada and Alaska, activity within the auroral oval intensifies the ionosphere's impact (by causing increased scintillation) on GPS signals passing through the ionosphere. You can

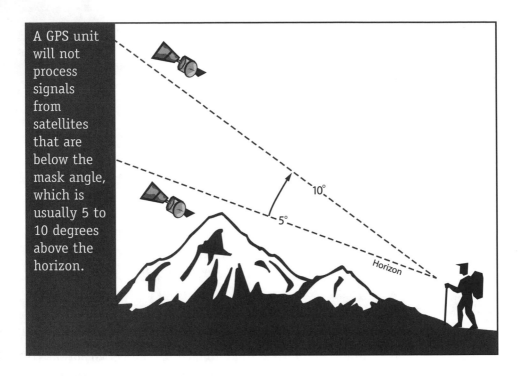

A GPS unit will not process signals from satellites that are below the mask angle, which is usually 5 to 10 degrees above the horizon.

assess the projected location of the area of auroral oval by clicking on the NOAA/TIROS Hemispheric Power Input Plot link at the Web site on the previous page. You can also take a peek at the site's Proton Flux Plot to get an idea of potential signal error related to bursts of solar energy.

Less mind numbing, and generally less pervasive (but just as real), are geophysical objects—natural and man-made—that block, reflect, or otherwise dilute a signal's precision.

A clear 360-degree view of the horizon and a cloudless sky are the keys to strong, steady signal reception. However, that scenario is more the exception than the rule. Physical barriers that block satellite signals include canyon walls, tall buildings, mountains, and hills. Under certain circumstances, the GPS unit will be unable to lock on to any signals— say, if you're inside a slot canyon or a narrow river gorge. For a satellite to be usable, it must be above the mask angle of the receiver. For example, most units will not process data from a GPS satellite that is no more than five degrees above the horizon.

In situations where you are unable to maintain a lock on at least three satellites (which results in a less desirable two-dimensional position fix; four satellites give you a three-dimensional position fix), the

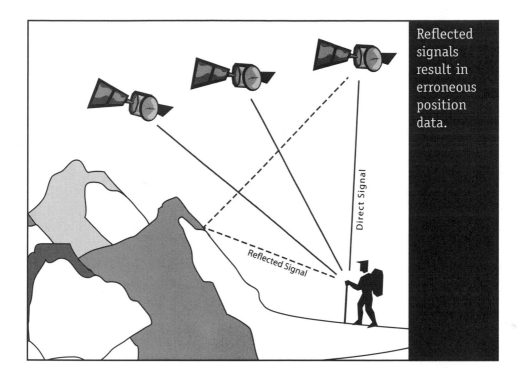

Reflected signals result in erroneous position data.

Direct Signal

Reflected Signal

unit will indicate that the signal has been lost. When you enter an area where reception is regained, as indicated by the receiver, drop a waypoint. By the end of a 10-mile hike through a narrow canyon, you may have the opportunity to drop several waypoints for reference.

False positioning is also possible when you're passing through canyons or near large walls and buildings. Normally, the satellite signals reach the receiver via a direct path. For the unit to accurately calculate your position, the direct signal path must be maintained. Occasionally, though, signals may reflect back to the receiver, creating an erroneous track log.

System Error

THE PRIMARY components of the GPS system are the constellation of satellites and the handheld unit. Ground stations that monitor satellite activity are critical to maintaining the system but are virtually out of mind as much as the satellites are out of sight. In other words, you can't see the satellites or the ground stations, but you do find yourself very aware of the satellites orbiting above the earth.

The U.S. Department of Defense keeps a minimum of 24 GPS satellites running and orbiting at the proper altitude. If a satellite goes down or

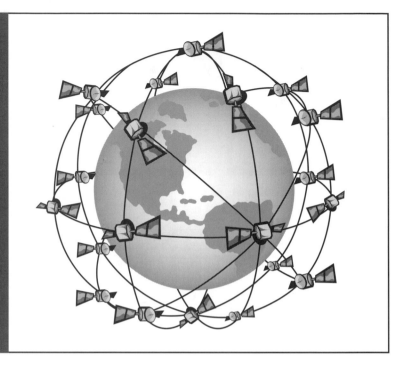

The GPS satellite constellation is made up of 24 GPS satellites.

must be repaired, spares are kept in orbit to take up the slack. If you are curious about the current health of the satellites, have had trouble locking on to signals on a particular day, or have a navigational mission that is of critical importance, you can access past, current, and future status information about each satellite at the U.S. Coast Guard NAVCEN Web site. By signing up to the NANU mailing list, you can automatically receive e-mail updates of changes made to the GPS constellation. To check on recent changes, another mailing list is available. Visit **www.navcen.uscg.gov/gps/subscribe.htm** for more information.

The most common source of system error is poor satellite geometry. The orbits of the satellites can be and often are changed to optimize signal reception in a specific region, usually in response to a combat situation or intelligence-gathering mission. An increase in signal precision in one area will result in a dilution of precision (DOP) in another. Ideally, when you boot up your unit, you'll lock on to four strong signals, one from directly overhead and the other three spaced evenly around the horizon, above the mask angle (see page 64). Poor satellite geometry will increase your position error and contribute to complete or intermittent signal loss. Odds are that on any particular day the geometry will serve you well, but there is a possibility that it will fail you—another reason to be prepared with a backup map and compass.

Other than poor satellite geometry or satellite malfunctions, which are out of our control, the only system component you should worry about is your GPS unit. In more than five years of using various GPS units, I've never had a single unit fail. Batteries have died, heavily clouded skies and canyon walls have obscured signals, but the units have functioned brilliantly.

The satellite system itself, being so critical to national-defense systems, is probably the least likely source of signal error.

ENJOYING YOUR GPS DATA

KEEPING IN MIND potential errors in your track and waypoint data, you can make maps and create an elevation profile of your journey along with attendant statistics, such as total elevation gain. Using the elevation profile, you can pinpoint exact mileage of key places such as crux turns or water sources. Thus, instead of writing in your blog, "Hike a couple of miles and look for a big rock on your left," you could write, "From the trailhead sign, walk 2.18 miles. Look to your left for a large car-sized boulder and a broken signpost. Continue for 1.6 miles and turn left onto a faint trail marked by a wooden post."

If you have Google Earth (**earth.google.com**) and a map program that interfaces with it (such as GPS Trackmaker), you can have the pleasure of watching your weekend forest loop zoom up at you. The program plots both track and waypoints over aerial and satellite imagery. With Google Earth you can also overlay roads and road labels to create a spectacular sight. A similar result can be achieved with DeLorme's TopoUSA (**www.delorme.com/topousa**), which allows you to download (for a fee) aerial photos and satellite images that correspond to the area covered by your adventure.

Just like a photo, the images created and data captured using your GPS unit provide a visual record of your outdoor pursuits and serve as a reference for future trips.

GLOSSARY

2D Operating Mode

A two-dimensional GPS position fix that includes only horizontal coordinates (no GPS elevation). It requires a minimum of three visible satellites.

3D Operating Mode

A three-dimensional GPS position fix that includes horizontal coordinates, plus elevation. It requires a minimum of four visible satellites.

Accuracy

A measure of how close an estimate of a GPS position is to the true location.

Acquisition Time

The time it takes a GPS receiver to acquire satellite signals and determine the initial position.

Active Antenna

An antenna that amplifies the GPS signal before sending it to the receiver.

Active Leg

The segment of a route currently being traveled. A *segment* is that portion of a route between any two waypoints in the route.

Almanac Data

Information transmitted by each satellite on the orbits and state (health) of every satellite in the GPS constellation. Almanac data allows the GPS receiver to rapidly acquire satellites shortly after it is turned on.

Altimeter

An instrument for determining elevation, especially an aneroid barometer used in aircraft that senses pressure changes accompanying changes in altitude.

Anti-spoofing

Encryption of the P code to protect the P signals from being "spoofed" through the transmission of false GPS signals by an adversary.

Atomic Clock

A very precise clock that operates using the elements cesium or rubidium. A cesium clock has an error of one second per million years. GPS satellites contain multiple cesium and rubidium clocks.

Azimuth

The horizontal direction from one point on the earth to another, measured clockwise in degrees (0 to 360) from a north or south reference line. An azimuth is also called a bearing.

Base Map

Many GPS units come with permanently built-in base maps, which typically include coverage of oceans, rivers, and lakes; principal cities, smaller cities, and towns; interstates, highways, and local thoroughfares; and railroads, airports, and political boundaries. Base maps are available in a variety of global coverage areas, depending on the user's needs.

Bearing

The compass direction from a position to a destination, measured to the nearest degree (also call an azimuth). In a GPS receiver, bearing usually refers to the direction to a waypoint.

Carrier Frequency

The frequency of an unmodulated output of a radio transmitter. The GPS L1 carrier frequency is 1575.42 MHz.

Coarse/Acquisition (C/A) Code

The standard positioning signal the GPS satellite transmits to the civilian user. It contains the information the GPS receiver uses to fix its position and time, and is accurate to 100 meters or better.

Cold Start

The power-on sequence whereby the GPS receiver downloads almanac data before establishing a position fix.

Control Segment

A worldwide chain of monitoring and control stations that control and manage the GPS satellite constellation.

Coordinates

A set of numbers that describe your location on or above the earth. Coordinates are typically based on latitude–longitude lines of reference or a global/regional grid projection such as UTM.

Coordinated Universal Time (UTC)

Replaced Greenwich Mean Time (GMT) as the world standard for time in 1986. UTC uses atomic-clock measurements to add or omit leap seconds each year to compensate for changes in the rotation of the earth.

Course

The direction from the beginning landmark of a course to its destination (measured in degrees, radians, or mils), or the direction from a route waypoint to the next waypoint in the route segment.

Course-deviation Indicator (CDI)

A technique for displaying the amount and direction of cross-track error (XTE).

Course Made Good (CMG)

The bearing from the "active from" position (your starting point) to your present position.

Course over Ground (COG)

Your direction of movement relative to a ground position.

Course to Steer

The heading you need to maintain in order to reach a destination.

Course-up Orientation

Fixes the GPS receiver's map display so the direction of navigation is always "up."

Cross-track Error (XTE/XTK)

The distance you are off the desired course in either direction.

Datum

A mathematical model that depicts a part of the surface of the earth. Latitude and longitude lines on a paper map are referenced to a specific map datum. The map datum selected on a GPS receiver needs to match the datum listed on the corresponding paper map in order for position readings to match.

Desired Track (DTK)

The compass course between the "from" and "to" waypoints.

Differential GPS (DGPS)

An extension of the GPS system that uses land-based radio beacons to transmit position corrections to GPS receivers. DGPS reduces the effect of selective availability, propagation delay, etc., and can improve position accuracy to better than 10 meters.

Dilution of Precision (DOP)

A measure of the GPS receiver/satellite geometry. A low DOP value indicates better relative geometry and higher corresponding accuracy. The DOP indicators are GDOP (geometric DOP), PDOP (position DOP), HDOP (horizontal DOP), VDOP (vertical DOP), and TDOP (time-clock offset).

Distance

The length (in feet, meters, miles, etc.) between two waypoints or from your current position to a destination waypoint. This length can be measured in straight-line (rhumb line) or great-circle (over the earth) terms. GPS normally uses great-circle calculations for distance and desired track.

DOD

The U.S. Department of Defense. The DOD manages and controls the Global Positioning System.

Downlink

A transmission path for the communication of signals and data from a communications satellite or other space vehicle to the earth.

Elevation

The distance above or below mean sea level.

Ephemeris Data

Current satellite position and timing information transmitted as part of the satellite data message. A set of ephemeris data is valid for several hours.

Estimated Position Error (EPE)

A measurement of horizontal position error in feet or meters based upon a variety of factors including DOP and satellite signal quality.

Estimated Time En Route (ETE)

The time it will take to reach your destination (in hours/minutes or minutes/seconds) based upon your present position, speed, and course.

Estimated Time of Arrival (ETA)

The estimated time you will arrive at a destination.

Frequency

The number of repetitions per unit time of a complete waveform, as of a radio wave (see L1 Frequency and L2 Frequency in this glossary).

Geocaching

A high-tech version of hide-and-seek. Geocachers seek out hidden treasures using GPS coordinates posted on the Internet by those hiding the cache.

Geodetic Datum

A mathematical model representing the size and shape of the earth (or a portion of it).

Geographic Information System (GIS)

A computer system or software capable of assembling, storing, manipulating, and displaying geographically referenced information (i.e., data identified according to its location). In practical use, GIS often refers to the computer system, software, data-collection equipment, personnel, and actual data.

Geosynchronous Orbit

A specific orbit around which a satellite rotates at the same rotational speed as the earth. A satellite rotating in geosynchronous orbit appears to remain stationary when viewed from a point on or near the equator. It is also referred to as a *geostationary orbit*.

Global Positioning System (GPS)

A global navigation system based on 24 or more satellites orbiting the earth at an altitude of 12,000 statute miles and providing very precise worldwide positioning and navigation information 24 hours a day, in any weather. Also called the NAVSTAR system.

GLONASS

The Global Orbiting Navigational Satellite System; the Russian counterpart to the United States' GPS system.

GoTo

A route consisting of one leg, with your present position being the start of the route and a single defined waypoint as the destination.

Greenwich Mean Time (GMT)

The mean solar time for Greenwich, England, which is located on the prime meridian (zero longitude). Based on the rotation of the earth, GMT is used as the basis for calculating standard time throughout most of the world.

Grid

A pattern of regularly spaced horizontal and vertical lines forming square zones on a map, such as the UTM system, used as a reference for establishing points.

Heading

The direction in which you are moving. For air and sea operations, this may differ from actual Course Over Ground (COG) due to winds, currents, etc.

Health

A term that describes an orbiting GPS satellite's suitability for use. Also referred to as the satellite's *state*.

Initialization

The first time a GPS receiver orients itself to its current location and collects almanac data. After initialization has occurred, the receiver remembers its location and acquires a position more quickly because it knows which satellites to look for.

Invert Route

To display and navigate a route from end to beginning for purposes of returning to the route's starting point.

Ionosphere

A region of the earth's atmosphere where ionization caused by incoming solar radiation affects the transmission of GPS radio waves. It extends from a height of 50 kilometers (30 miles) to 400 kilometers (250 miles) above the surface.

L1 Frequency

One of the two radio frequencies transmitted by the GPS satellites. This frequency carries the C/A code, P code, and nav message, and is transmitted on a frequency of 1575.42 MHz.

L2 Frequency

One of the two radio frequencies transmitted by the GPS satellites. This frequency carries only the P code and is transmitted on a frequency of 1227.6 MHz.

L Band

The radio frequencies that extend from 390 MHz to 1550 MHz. The GPS carrier frequencies are in the L band (1227.6 MHz and 1575.42 MHz).

Latitude

A position's distance north or south of the equator, measured by degrees from zero to 90. One minute of latitude equals one nautical mile.

Leg (Route)

A portion of a route consisting of a starting (from) waypoint and a destination (to) waypoint. A route that is composed of waypoints A, B, C, and D would contain three legs. The route legs would be from A to B, from B to C, and from C to D.

Liquid Crystal Display (LCD)

A display circuit characterized by a liquid crystal element sandwiched between two glass panels. Characters are produced by applying an electric field to liquid crystal molecules and arranging them to act as light filters.

Local Area Augmentation System (LAAS)

The implementation of ground-based DGPS to support aircraft landings in a local area (20-mile range).

Longitude

The distance east or west of the prime meridian (measured in degrees). The prime meridian runs from the North Pole to the South Pole through Greenwich, England.

LORAN

LORAN, which stands for LOng RAnge Navigation, is a grid of radio waves in many areas of the globe that allows accurate position plotting. LORAN transmitting stations around the globe continually transmit 100-kHz radio signals. Special shipboard LORAN receivers interpret these signals and provide readings that correspond to a grid overprinted on nautical charts. By comparing signals from two different stations, the mariner uses the grid to determine the position of the vessel.

Magnetic North

Represents the direction of the north magnetic pole from the observer's position. The direction in which a compass points.

Magnetic Variation

In navigation, at a given place and time, the horizontal angle (or difference) between true north and magnetic north. Magnetic variation is measured east or west of true north.

Mean Sea Level

The average level of the ocean's surface, as measured by the level halfway between mean high and low tide. Used as a standard in determining land elevation or sea depths.

Multipath Error

An error caused when a satellite signal reaches the GPS receiver antenna by more than one path. Usually caused by one or more paths being bounced or reflected. The TV equivalent of multipath is "ghosting."

Multiplexing Receiver

A GPS receiver that switches at a very rapid rate between satellites being tracked. Typically, multiplexing receivers require more time for satellite acquisition and are not as accurate as parallel-channel GPS receivers. Multiplexing receivers are also more prone to lose a satellite fix in dense woods than parallel-channel receivers.

Nautical Mile

A unit of length used in sea and air navigation, based on the length of one minute of arc of a great circle, especially an international and U.S. unit equal to 1,852 meters (about 6,076 feet).

Navigation

The act of determining the course or heading of movement. This movement could be for a plane, ship, automobile, person on foot, or the like.

Navigation Message

The message transmitted by each GPS satellite containing system time, clock-correction parameters, ionospheric-delay-model parameters, and the satellite's ephemeris data and health. The information is used to process GPS signals to give the user time, position, and velocity. Also known as the *data message*.

NAVSTAR

The official U.S. Government name given to the GPS satellite system. NAVSTAR is an acronym for NAVigation Satellite Timing And Ranging.

NMEA (National Marine Electronics Association)

A U.S. standards committee that defines data message structure, contents, and protocols to allow the GPS receiver to communicate with other pieces of electronic equipment aboard ships.

NMEA Standard

A NMEA standard defines an electrical interface and data protocol for communications among marine instrumentation.

North-up Orientation

Fixes the GPS receiver's map display so north is always fixed at the top of the screen.

Parallel-channel Receiver

A continuous-tracking receiver using multiple receiver circuits to track more than one satellite simultaneously.

P Code

The precise code of the GPS signal, typically used only by the U.S. military. It is encrypted and reset every seven days to prevent use by unauthorized persons.

Position

An exact, unique location based on a geographic-coordinate system.

Position Fix

The GPS receiver's computed position coordinates.

Position Format

The way in which the GPS receiver's position is displayed on the screen. Commonly displayed as latitude–longitude in degrees and minutes, with options for degrees, minutes and seconds, degrees only, and one of several grid formats.

Prime Meridian

The zero meridian, used as a reference line from which longitude east and west is measured. It passes through Greenwich, England.

Quadrifilar Helix Antenna

A type of GPS antenna in which four spiraling elements form the receiving surface of the antenna. For GPS use, quadrifilar antennas are typically half-wavelength or quarter-wavelength size and encased in a plastic cylinder for durability.

Route

A group of waypoints entered into the GPS receiver in the sequence you desire to navigate them.

Selective Availability (SA)

The random error that the government can intentionally add to GPS signals so their accuracy for civilian use is degraded. SA is not currently in use.

Speed over Ground (SOG)

The actual speed at which the GPS unit is moving over the ground. This may differ from airspeed or nautical speed because of such things as head winds or sea conditions. For example, a plane that is going 120 knots into a 10-knot head wind will have a SOG of 110 knots.

Statute Mile

A unit of length equal to 5,280 feet or 1,760 yards (1,609 meters), used in the United States and some other English-speaking countries.

Straight-line Navigation

The act of going from one waypoint to another in the most direct line and with no turns.

Time to First Fix (TTFF)

If you have not used your GPS unit for several months, the almanac data for the satellites may be out-of-date. The unit is capable of recollecting this information on its own, but the process can take several minutes. Time to First Fix (TTFF) is the time it takes a GPS receiver to find satellites after the user first turns it on (when the GPS receiver has lost memory or has been moved more than 300 miles from its last location).

Track (TRK)

Your current direction of travel relative to a ground position (same as Course over Ground).

Track-up Orientation

Fixes the GPS receiver's map display so the current track heading is at the top of the screen.

Triangulation

A method of determining the location of an unknown point, as in GPS navigation, by using the laws of plane trigonometry.

Troposphere

The lowest region of the atmosphere between the surface of the earth and the tropopause, characterized by decreasing temperature with increasing altitude. GPS signals travel through the troposphere and other atmospheric layers.

True North

The direction of the North Pole from your current position. Magnetic compasses indicate north differently because of the variation between true north and magnetic north. A GPS receiver can display headings referenced to true north or magnetic north.

Turn (TRN)

The degrees that must be added to or subtracted from the current heading to reach the course to the intended waypoint.

Universal Transverse Mercator (UTM)

A nearly worldwide coordinate-projection system using north and east distance measurements from reference point(s). UTM is the primary coordinate system used for U.S. Geological Survey topographic maps.

Uplink

A transmission path by which radio or other signals are sent from the ground to an aircraft or a communications satellite.

User Interface

The way in which information is exchanged between the GPS receiver and the user—specifically, the screen display and buttons on the unit.

User Segment

The segment of the complete GPS system that includes the GPS receiver and operator.

Velocity Made Good (VMG)

The rate of closure to a destination based upon your current speed and course.

Waypoints

Waypoints are locations or landmarks worth recording and storing in your GPS. These are locations you may later want to return to. They may be checkpoints on a route or significant ground features (e.g., camp, a truck, a fork in a trail, or a favorite fishing spot). Waypoints may be defined and stored in the unit manually by taking coordinates for the waypoint from a map or other reference. You can do this before you ever leave home. More usually, waypoints may be entered directly by taking a reading with the unit at the location itself, giving it a name, and then saving the point. Waypoints may also be put into the unit by referencing another waypoint already stored, giving the reference waypoint, and entering the distance and compass bearing to the new waypoint.

Wide Area Augmentation System (WAAS)

A system of satellites and ground stations that provides GPS signal corrections for better position accuracy. A WAAS-capable receiver can give you a position accuracy of better than three meters 95 percent of the time. (At this time, the system is still in the development stage and is not fully operational.) WAAS consists of approximately 25 ground reference stations positioned across the United States that monitor GPS satellite data. Two master stations, located on either coast, collect data from the reference stations and create a GPS correction message.

WGS-84

World Geodetic System, 1984. The primary map datum used by GPS. Secondary datums are computed as differences from the WGS 84 standard.

Y Code

Encrypted P code.

INDEX

Page numbers for figures and diagrams are shown in **Bold.**